STEP OUT

Release Your Inner Greatness

An Anthology by Busy Working Mothers

FOR

Busy Working Mothers

Compiled by

OMOWUNMI OLUNLOYO

With a collection, of

AMAZING, BOLD & COURAGEOUS MOTHERS

Step Out: Release Your Inner Greatness

copyright © 2017 Omowunmi Olunloyo and contributing authors

First published as a collection -------JULY 2017

978-0-9957349-3-7 (eBook)

978-0-9957349-2-0 (Paperback)

Cover design by Robert Nimako Brefo

All Rights Reserved.

No part of this book may be reproduced in any form or by any electronic or mechanical means, including storage and retrieval systems, without written permission from the publisher, except in the case of a reviewer, who may quote brief passages embodied in critical articles or a review.

The publisher does not have any control over and does not assume any responsibility for author or third-party websites and their content.

Disclaimer

This book is to educate and provide general information. The reader is advised to consult with their advisor regarding their specific situation. The author and compiler have taken reasonable precautions in the preparation of this book and believes that the facts presented were accurate at the time of writing. The author and compiler do not assume any responsibility for error or omissions. The author and compiler specifically disclaim any liability resulting from the use or application of the information contained in the book.

Book Projects proudly features writers from all over the English-speaking world. Some speak and write English as their first language, while for others, it's their second, third or even fourth language. Naturally, across all versions of English, there are differences in punctuation and spelling, and even in meaning. These differences are reflected in the work Book Projects publishes, and it accounts for any differences in punctuation, spelling and meaning found within these pages.

PRAISE FOR STEP OUT

Step Out is an inspirational story of how a woman overcame self-doubt and learnt to love herself for who she truly is.

Natasha Dykes, Professional Network Marketer

Step Out is a journey from darkness, courageously stepping out of the shadow and into the truth and integrity of who we are. It's about perseverance, determination, love and hope. It's about turning our mess into our success. And ultimately, it's about faith. Because when you trust the process, divinity favours the brave. An inspiring read to encourage us all to step out and into our greatness.

Michelle Catanach, Transformational Book Coach for visionaries, revolutionaries, creatives and conscious entrepreneurs

Omowunmi speaks from the heart and is an inspiration to all women in need of support and permission. She tells the story of all women as they struggle to life a life of congruence with who they truly are. When she writes "Women, do not be afraid. Be focused be determined. Be hopeful. Be empowered. Empower yourselves with a good education, then get out there and use that knowledge to build an environment, a community, a society worthy of your boundless promise." she is speaking from experience, compassion and love.

Becky Hess, CEO, Bhess Group

Step Out is a collection of courageous authors, who share their real and raw stories of overwhelm, pain, challenge and triumph. Women all over the world will be able to relate to the author's stories, as they come from many backgrounds and continents. Their stories give the reader hope and help to inspire them, that no matter what they are facing in their lives, they are not alone! Other women have faced similar challenges, have come through them, and are now thriving. Reading this book is akin to having tea with a group of busy, working moms, sharing stories and swapping advice and ideas. It's a must read!

Lisa Petr, Zen Virtual Assistant Services

"This story touched my heart, even put tears on my eyes. It is an amazing story full of emotions, fight and faith. We have a lot to learn about this. Just love it and make me admire and respect more than ever her lovely author. "

Toks, oh my God! Good job my sister! Well done! And thank you so much for sharing it with me.

Laura Buxo, International Best-Selling Author of Love Unboxed

An inspiring evergreen book for mothers. You will not want to drop it until the last page.

Adebimpe Adeniyi-Fashina, Cancer Data Administrator, Mother of 3 Amazing Kings.

DEDICATION

"The two most important days in your life are the day you are born and the day you find out why." - Mark Twain

This book is dedicated to busy working mothers everywhere who have found their place, position and purpose and occupied it, thereby paving a way for other busy working mothers to know without a shadow of a doubt that it is possible to live the life you have dreamt of as a woman, wife and working mother.

My intention is that Step Out! Release Your Inner Greatness book transforms your life and causes a massive impact such that when you look back one year from now, you would be able to see better results in your life.

"I believe each of us has a mission in life, and that one cannot truly be living their most fulfilled life until they recognize this mission and dedicate their life to pursuing it." - Blake Mycoskie

TABLE OF CONTENTS

Dedication	v
Foreword by Mayowa Ijisesan	ix
Introduction	1

Part One: One Step Forward 3

Omowunmi Olunloyo - Still Standing 5

Adeola Olayinka - Seasons and Lessons 15

Ebun Bilankulu- Breaking Free From Expectation And Looking Forward 27

Ibukunoluwa E. Ogunbola (aka Ibikay)- Finding Me After The Storm 35

Part Two: Forge Ahead 47

Morenike Asaju- The Place 49

Adetola Ogbebor- Life Is Not A Dress Rehearsal 61

Kelle Wares- Learning the Meaning of Serenity 69

Tutu Ademola (aka TU2) - An Enjoyable Challenge 81

STEP OUT

Part Three: Breaking The Rules **91**

Adetola Ty Tamunokubie- Grass To Grace 93

Dr Mary Pellicer- From Doctor to Healer, My Journey of Discovery 101

Agnese Osemwegie- This Is My Story 115

Franscica Okin- My Journey So Far 129

Part Four: Making My Mark **135**

The Purpose Driven Lady- Olajumoke Poku 137

Diary of a Purpose Driven Lady with Bukola Oragbade 141

Aminat Alli -My Beautiful Scar 147

Conclusion **153**

About the Compiler **155**

Other Resources **157**

More Books by Omowunmi Olunloyo **159**

About the Publisher **163**

About our Books: **165**

FOREWORD BY MAYOWA IJISESAN

Women face a lot these days. They face so much pressure to be the woman, mother, wife, professional or minister that they need to be. Sometimes, it may feel like being pulled in a hundred different directions. It is a lot to be confronted with daily and there is nothing worse than facing this with, not just a feeling of inadequacy, but also a sense that we are going through day-in and day-out without experiencing much change or growth ourselves. Change is good. A sense of growth is great. Knowing that one matter and that the contribution that one makes counts is very empowering. Nobody wants to keep running the rat race without much internal growth or progress.

'Step Out' is a compilation of stories written by 15 amazing women who have found a way to break out of the cycle and create purposeful, meaningful lives. They have found a way to overcome the frustrations and stress. In this book, they share their inspiring stories.

I am happy Omowunmi Olunloyo has invested in putting the time, effort and energy into compiling these stories into a book that is sure to inspire you and bring some needed change in your life. I love the creativity with which this book has been put together. The format is engaging, relatable and very real. These stories are of struggle to triumph; of stagnancy to progress; and of frustration to stress free living.

This book will be a blessing to you. If you are a busy, working mother in need of change, it was especially written with you in mind. So, sit back, relax, grab something to sip on and enjoy the book – 'Step Out – Release Your Inner Greatness'

INTRODUCTION

15 Busy Working Mothers

This book is about busy working mothers who have found a way to live their best life inspite of all the challenges she has faced as a woman, wife and working mother.

The book aims to inspire, challenge and encourage busy working mothers all around the world to step out; to be bold and courageous, to stop settling, and manifest their awesomeness because the world is awaiting.

You will find a connection as you read through the pages of real life journeys of busy working mothers just like you who stepped out to release their inner greatness.

These busy working mothers have committed to sharing not only successes, wins and triumph but their struggles, sorrows and sacrifices they have made; in the hopes that you will see yourself as you read through the pages and realise you are not alone so that you can embrace your purpose and stop excusing yourself from living the life you know you are supposed to live.

"I believe that each of us has our path to follow. If we are walking this path, things flow, and we feel energised and happy". - Sarah O' Flaherty

Part One:
One Step Forward

Omowunmi Olunloyo - Still Standing

L ife was hard for me. People did not know that I was lonely and sad. That was then. This is now.

Now I am happy, loved and life is great.

"Accept yourself, love yourself, and keep moving forward. If you want to fly, you have to give up what weighs you down."
   - Roy T. Bennett

The beginning

I was at the darkest point of my life in 2011; it seems like such a long time ago now. I was in the valley. I tried desperately to understand everything that was going on. This season felt like forever, my world was crashing down on me. Each element of my existence was falling apart, one by one and it appeared like there was nothing I could do to stop it. I could not change it. I felt so helpless and hopeless.

My life journey was a roller coaster ride, with low and high moments and challenges that I could not control.

One of my greatest challenges was accepting that I was enough, that I was good enough just the way I was. Instead of trying to be somebody I wasn't.

I sacrificed my true purpose for fear of rejection, abandonment, and loneliness. I struggled with low self-esteem and fitting in with the crowd. I could not see past my shortcomings, I felt like a loser. My relationship was affected; I was disrespected, separated, and abused. Called every kind of name under the sun and my self-worth was next to none. I attended all kinds of programs and training to prove to myself that I was good enough and should be recognised. I thought I was unattractive and I wanted to change all of that. I did not love myself.

I wanted to understand everything that led me to believe that I was not good enough. Did it have to do with the way I was brought up? What had happened in my life to affect me so much now?

Nigeria

I grew up in a beautiful neighborhood in Lagos Nigeria with my two sisters. I was raised by my parents who were very disciplined and principled. Both of my parents are well educated. They were what you would desire parents to be, hardworking, patient, believe the best of you and very loving. My parents, especially my dad is often referred to as "Baba o", which is translated as "my father" by young and old. He was everybody's friend. He was fun, full of life, happy and a very generous giver. My parents expected the best from us, always reminding and encouraging us to go higher.

I spent my childhood making memories of many happy moments. When I started secondary school, I was excited. I was just ten years old. I began to experience different encounters that challenged who I was. I tried my best to fit in and join the crowd as much as I could.

As I moved from one class year to another, I experienced different issues no matter what I did. I was not good enough. I was not accepted as part of the crew. Do not get me wrong; despite all I faced, I had a few friends. They are still friends today and they accepted me as me. At that time, I did not know what they saw in me, but in hindsight I realised there was more to me that meets the eye. Also, towards the end of my secondary school I was ill. I spent several weeks in and out of hospital recovering, which was a horrible event in my life.

College, failed relationship and marriage

Despite the various challenges in my senior high school, I completed it and got admission into college. Life became good again. I made new friends and I enjoyed my time at my new college. Everything was going great. I was happy again.

I also started a relationship that was supposed to lead to marriage. After 2 and a half years it ended abruptly. There was no reason or explanation given. I was devastated as you can imagine. Another rejection I could not explain.

My self-esteem was knocked back, and I began to struggle again. But somehow, I found a way to love again and I entered my second relationship and got married after four years.

For some reason, I thought that because I was now an"MRS.", All the issues I had been dealing with would go away. Boy, was I wrong. The shock I felt as I began to live as a married woman was undeniable. I dreamed of a fairy tale world where everyone lived happily ever after. My true life was not like this. I struggled to find my place, position, and purpose without my spouse. I could not see how I could do anything without him.

My journal

During this period of my life, I found journaling and began to write more frequently. I wrote almost every day about everything that rocked my world, the following extracts are taken from it:

"Do not faint, your time for reward is here keep at it". This was spoken to me in January 2013 by one of my mentors. I received the word, but did not see how that could happen. I believed in the faith he had in the words he said to me.

"Lord, you know all, and see the heart of everybody, nothing is hid from your sight. I feel out of place, I am not comfortable, I want to serve but I am not used, it appears as if I am not needed. I am talked on and about, where is the love? I have been told not to take offense, help me Lord. I need you more than ever. I am lost I need your arms all around me; I want to feel your love right now. Speak to me. If you can use anything Lord you can use me". I wrote this at a time when I was about to give up on everything and I turned to my Lord for help.

In 2014, I wrote "Lord, I am not happy right now, I am being told I say things they way they are. I feel hurt and disappointed about the feedback. I feel targeted now. I am not pleased. I choose to leave it all to you".

I carried out a purpose quiz online in 2015, as part of finding myself. I was beginning to love myself and this was the assessment I got back:

Life is good. You have seen some real breakthrough in your life and you are ready to begin living at the highest levels of the purpose pyramid! It's clear that you have a good understanding of what you want from life and have skills and experience to help you get there. You might not be fully aware of your purpose, or how to allow it to guide and enhance every aspect of your life. For you, there is still powerful unrealised potential.

I was excited at this point because, I was beginning to give myself a break and a chance. I was not being too hard on myself even though I was still battling with not being good enough. The assessment gave me hope.

My light bulb moment

After several years of trying to fit in, people pleasing, working hard, *really hard.* I experienced a light bulb moment. I renewed my mind, I listened to messages that uplifted and gave me hope. Gradually over time I became free to be, to do and have effortlessly and that is how my story changed. My favourite book reminded me that as I think in my heart so am I. I started to think happy thoughts so that my actions were powerful, pleasant, and positive. It is what I think that I become, this is how I transformed my life.

I took responsibility for my action. I began to consciously watch what I allowed to enter my life. I chose to operate by faith. I realised that unless I hear the words, faith will not come. I was committed to my faith, despite everything trying to stop me believing. Saying and doing is a lifestyle of a believer I was told, so since I believed I spoke. I speak to myself a lot, my friends can testify to this. My life is a demonstration of the proof that it is possible. I began to see a lot of value in myself. From no hope to having hope; and this hope translates to faith. I received the revelation in the words I heard and it made it easy to speak. It's about believing, ladies, that your action dictates your faith.

I cannot say one action transformed me; I believe it was an accumulation of very small actions that produced the better version of myself on display right now. I knew the change was coming, I knew I had to show up; I had to come out from the background, from the shadows, and shine brightly and be bold about it. Yes, I felt stuck; but I was ready to live in integrity with my values, not somebody's, not my friends not even society; I acted despite the fear I felt.

Steps to change

Allow me to share with you the steps I took to create my transformation. I decided to love myself, to accept that I was good enough and that I was beautiful. Love is such a powerful force. Then I told a few people about my new decision. I saw myself achieving my decision and I used a vision board to bring it to life. I created confessions or affirmations as some like to call it, which I declare daily. As I achieved my goal by taking little action steps I rewarded myself. This did something to my mind, I believed myself more, and it helped to reaffirm and reinforce my behaviour. For you to have faith you must hear and believe. I experienced the miraculous when I acted out my faith.

STEP OUT

I am more confident, proud, and I love myself so much, you would not believe it. This change in mindset and attitude produced tremendous results in the key core areas of my life. I have launched a weekend retreat program for women where they learn to rest and receive, started a coaching business, published my own magazine and guess who was the cover girl 3 times in a row, yours truly. I am a published author of 3 books with my latest book "Loved Unboxed" being a Best Seller in five countries and here I am again, a complier of my own anthology with fourteen amazing women sharing a message of hope and possibility. Doors are opening to me because I dared to believe that just maybe, I am that special, unique, different and that is absolutely fine. I am now a minister of enjoyment. I rest and receive.

Perhaps you are going through a similar situation, where you are scared, lonely and afraid but you know deep down inside that there is more to you than what you are currently going through or maybe you have gone through this road before and you are on your way to living fully and showing up, I want to motivate, empower, encourage, educate you. Know this: you are valuable, unique, special, different, one of a kind for a reason. Think about it for a moment, please indulge me, do you think you went through all this for nothing. Seriously, the heartache, the sleepless night, the abuse, loneliness? I do not think so. Are you going to trust your inner voice telling you to step out, to be, to do and have? Are you going to take your place and manifest your awesomeness? Are you?

STEP OUT

In times like this, when my faith is being tried and tested, how I respond defines me. Do I choose to stay afraid, timid, and hidden or do I believe the inner voice that is guiding me and trust it no matter what?

I thought to be different was a negative thing and I was afraid. But as I grew up, I realised being different is not a negative thing at all. We are all born to stand out; blending in would be so boring. Imagine how boring the world would be if everyone were the same. I believe each one of us has been put here for a reason and when you do not show up to occupy your spot, it affects lives that are connected to you. When you do not do the things you should be doing, you are missing the life you should be living and the impact it should be making.

Role models

My overall message to you is to be bold and courageous, to do something different, press on, do not give up or cave in. It is possible and yes you can. If you are alive, there is hope, you are not without hope no matter how bad it seems. I aim to encourage and remind you that no matter what you are going through right now, there is a light at the end of the tunnel.

And in closing in the words of the First lady of America Michelle Obama, at her final official emotional farewell speech, so for you reading right now, know that you are enough. Do not ever let make you feel like you do not matter or that you do not have a place, position, or purpose because you do. And you have a right to exactly who you are.

I want all women to know that they matter, that they belong, so do not be afraid. Do you hear me?

Women, do not be afraid. Be focused be determined. Be hopeful. Be empowered. Empower yourselves with a good education, then get out there and use that knowledge to build an environment, a community, a society worthy of your boundless promise. Lead by example with hope, never fear. And know that I'll be with you, rooting for you and working to support you for the rest of my life. And that is true, I know, for every co-author who is in this amazing book that gets up every day and works their hearts out to lift up other women.

And am so grateful to all of you for your passion, sense of purpose and your dedication. And I can think of no better way to end my story than celebrating you for taking the bold step to transform your life. So, I want to close by saying thank you. Thank you for believing in yourself enough to invest in your education, your personal development and growth. Being the complier of Step Out series is one of the greatest honour of my life and I hope I have inspired you and shined a torch of light and hope to you to enable you to Step Out and Release Your Inner Greatness.

Adeola Olayinka - Seasons and Lessons

"During those times, I learnt that the best gift you can give your children as a mum, no matter what you may be up against is not an education, not clothes, toys, or even food. The best gift you can give those beauties is you. TAKE CARE OF YOURSELF."
- Adeola Olayinka

Life comes in seasons, and understanding the season we are in goes a long way in helping us deal with the momentary occurrences that take place in our lives regardless of whether we perceive them to be positive or negative. Each season in life impacts the others since our take-off point in a new season is most likely impacted by our success in the last.

In recent years, I have come to look at my life as a flow, every experience bringing with it a life lesson which if learnt will come to impact later seasons of my life. My ability to successfully learn these lessons as I come along my path determines the quality of my life and the eventual strength of my personality.

I will like to share with you a few of my experiences and the lessons I have learnt along the way which have come to form a huge part of who I am; my strength, skill and even emotions.

Starting from my growing up years, it was a mixture of fun and work, more like learning responsibility. Being the only female child, I was my father's favourite and you would think that I would be spoiled but, in my opinion, I was the most disciplined of the four children my parents had. I guess my curious mind and my incessant questions were quite challenging. My parents did their best but just couldn't keep up with my thirst to know.

I remember my mum saying to me once out of frustration; "Don't ask any question that starts with how 'what', 'where', 'who' or 'when'." For a moment I was quiet, thinking how I was going to ask her how I was to ask questions without using any of the banned words! This experience helped me in relating to my daughter who can ask a thousand questions in a minute. I remember feeling the exact exasperation my mum must have felt years ago but it made me laugh so loud, I turned it into a story for my little five-year old (at the time). She got the message but in a subtle way and we jointly agreed it was important she came to me with every question she may have, however, we may need to put a timeline to get some answers.

Though I didn't realise it then, that experience with my mum birthed in me a patience needed to raise my highly inquisitive female child.

As a teenager and only girl, I cleaned, cooked and took care of the house, sometimes without much supervision. I could hold my own and run the household. My chores were mapped out for me by myself, and as far as I was concerned, if they weren't done, I couldn't eat. My mum always made sure I wrapped the gifts we gave out to people, picked out cards or set the table for family lunch, which happened more times in our home than in most at that time. That taught me to pay attention to details, developed my love for words and made giving gifts a skill that would come to be one of my survival tools in later years.

I have always enjoyed both my own company and that of others. I would sit alone in my room writing poems about my life, or life as I saw it through my innocent eyes; I would stay for hours drawing a picture to hang in my room or give to a friend. Sometimes, especially late in the evenings I would sit in a chosen spot in the compound (my father had a large one) and would sing my heart out. Looking back I am sure the neighbours must have cringed each time, but thankfully, no one complained so I just had my fill of my voice. Whitney Houston songs were the topmost on my list. I loved her to bits. She was one of my idols, her powerful voice, dark skin and beautiful eyes always lifted me. I sang her songs so much I earned the nickname 'Whitney' in school. That vocal gift was later used when I joined the choir. I remember having a music director who stretched me, telling me I could sing Shirley Caesar songs.

After joining the choir, I asked a friend how she was able to adlib to songs so well, it just made it all sound so lovely, and she said you have to sing 'Alto', (that's a musical part) I was singing 'Soprano' at the time. I asked to switch and got clearance from my director. I would listen as Ada sang and will practice a lot until I could stand by self to sing in part and then I learnt adlibbing too.

Each time I made it through, it made me see how easy it was to achieve the toughest tasks. ***Lesson learnt: you can achieve anything you set your heart to with determination and focus.***

In high school, I wasn't popular, or so I thought, I didn't think I mattered a lot to people. I moved from being bullied to becoming friends with the bully after standing my ground. I guess my tender nature gave people the idea that they could take advantage of me though I didn't realise it then. I had many close friends at different times in high school. Each term, someone else was close to me. The other person remained my friend but I just moved on to the next person that needed me the most I guess. Though I still didn't realise it, my friendships were based on what I could give to the other person. I remember there was a girl who was teased for being quiet, she used to have a lot of wax in her ears could see it just standing close to her, we became friends and all I wanted to do was help her clean her ears only to find out she had medical instructions not to. She was my closest friend for about two terms and I learnt how she managed her wax-filled ear and found what a sweetheart she was. This was useful to me years down the line when I had my daughter and she had 'waxy'-ears.

Let me say, in high school, I had to repeat a class. I was a part of a set that was a year ahead of me in age and as much as I tried to fit in, I didn't. In my junior transitory exam to the senior classes, I flunked my national exams and had to stay back. That was when I started enjoying high school. I remember my dad telling me during the holidays before I joined the class I was repeating into, that I should forget I was ever a part of the other set but just face this new one, I shouldn't see myself as their senior but as their mates because that's what I was now. I followed that advice, got ridiculed for it by my old mates but I didn't care, that counsel sat well with me and I followed it headlong. I can say it paid off.

Years later, over twenty years later in fact, I began to

learn from my colleagues in school how much my words impacted their lives and how I helped them through many tough decisions. That was news to me, because I didn't think I mattered so much. I remember a friend of mine, a little over a year now, telling me after we reconnected how she searched for me to apologise for treating me badly in school, she had left me a message on Facebook and I never responded so she thought I was still upset. Wow! First off, I knew she did pick on me, though she was my friend and I loved her too, but I couldn't even remember one thing she did and I never saw the message she sent to me. We are still friends now. This was one of many to come.

So I moved from being the girl that thought she didn't matter to the girl that had touched lives but didn't realize it until twenty years after.

This taught me two lessons:

1. ***What people say or do is limited by their understanding at the time so excuse their misgivings and love them still.***

2. ***You never really know how much impact your words, actions or attitude have on others so be careful what seeds you sow.***

After secondary school, I gained admission into a polytechnic, I didn't like it but my dad didn't want me out of state, though I wanted to get away from home so bad. Both schools I picked in my university choices were out of state. So I stayed home and I didn't like that much. It was while I was in my first year that I sat one day on the railings in front of my lecture room and I was deep in thoughts, my closet friend then was sitting by me and I looked up at her and said:

"Okay, so after school we work, marry, have kids, grow old… then what?" I remember her looking up at me like I was crazy to even think such thoughts. Then I said "There has to be more to life than this…" At that point I began to desire to know for myself the essence of life and in my quest, I found Christ and surrendered my life to him. My faith in God has come to mean everything to me. From it I draw strength, inspiration, and life. Without my faith, no lesson in life, relationship or achievement will mean much. That day on the railing, I asked the question that would set the rest of my life on course.

While most of my friends spent money on clothes, hair and make-up, I invested in books. I always had a book in hand and I always enjoyed just lying back to read a book. Most books I read were Christian literature and they helped to form who I am today. Authors like Kenneth Hagin, Watchman Nee, Joyce Meyer, Frank Perreti, Max Lucado and so many others.

As I became older, now in my twenties, I became a part of a youth fellowship where I learnt to stand with people and to stand alone in faith. Those two years gave me tools that would help me navigate tough tides in life as time went on. I learnt the way of faith. I learnt that God is my only source and that the only problem I can ever have in life is me. I came to understand that if I believe all that the Lord says to me in His Word (the bible) and in who he says I am, then I am more than equipped to overcome any challenge I come face to face with in life. That lesson helped me through the darkest times of my life and still is propelling me daily to face the challenges that raising children alone in a very economically hostile environment can bring.

I got married and had two children; a son and a daughter. Then life happened and I found myself divorced. Where I come from, a woman in this state is not smiled at. I remember how scared I was when I started on this path. I didn't have money, I had lost my self-worth and didn't have friends who still came around. All I had was my two children, N20,000 (less than 100 dollars), a teaching job which owed me for two months, a supportive family and my faith. I remember reading a book titled "Raising Great Kids on Your Own" by David & Lisa Frisbie. I devoured the book and set out on my journey, very uncertain and very afraid of what the future held.

There were nights I cried myself to sleep and days I didn't want to get out of bed. But I got up each morning because I had two children ages five and three to nurture. I put a smile on my face to shield them, because that is what we mum's do. We had fun, played, danced and ensured happy wasn't lost on us. If you didn't know me, you wouldn't know what was going on. During those times, I learnt that the best gift you can give your children as a mum, no matter what you may be up against is not an education, not clothes, toys, or even food. The best gift you can give those beauties is you. TAKE CARE OF YOURSELF.

You know how in the plane the pilot tells his passengers to wear their air mask before trying to put it on others, even if that other is a child? Yeah, that's how you take care of yourself first. The reason is when you are well, your children perceive it, and they are first of all stable psychologically and emotionally, then you can work through providing the clothes, toys and even food for them.

I would watch movies, soaps because they helped me keep sane and I learnt a lot from them. Two that strike me and I am grateful for are:

One Tree Hill and *Desperate Housewives*. Yes, I know right! What on earth did I learn from those soaps? Both soap operas taught me to appreciate:

1. ***The importance of relationships, especially friends.*** People come into our lives to help us through our journey as we help them through theirs too. I learnt from the characters as I watched, how having friends can make a huge difference in a person's life. It allowed me to open up to support from people around me. We all need to have a support system to walk this road, YOU CANNOT DO IT ALL BY YOURSELF! And I know

many of us are careful about who we leave our children with, who knows our business and so on. Truth is, we should care but within reason, to this I always say: LISTEN TO YOUR HEART. Don't be paranoid! If you are a good person, then there are billions of good people out there who will love and support you. Yes, with all your baggage. You will get hurt along the way that is a guarantee because people aren't perfect, none of us are, but even those hurtful experiences will bring lessons to help make a success of the next seasons of your life. Nothing is lost if you will count everything, good or not so good, all joy.

2. *Life is in seasons.* It was at this point in my life I learnt everything I have to share with you. It was here that I started appreciating the experiences of my life, stringing them together came much later. They were in the pits today, no direction, no hope then things begin to pick up and 'BOOM!'. I saw how through it all they took it a day at a time until they were strong enough to take the quantum leap that would shoot them into a brand-new season.

Life will always bring the tools that will help you navigate life as you know it, in the form of people, experiences, books, songs, movies, they can be in any guise, how you respond to them and employ them will help make things easier on you or otherwise.

There were days I made mistakes. Some seemed more grievous than others (or so I thought) but with every mistake, I leaned on God by faith through grace to carry me through. You know those life experiences I started appreciating? At some point I had some sessions with a life coach who helped me to string them together, both the good and the not-so-good, so that I begin to see the joys in every one of those balls.

Have you seen the animated movie 'Inside Out'? Every experience was on a ball that was carefully kept, some faded into oblivion after a while and some formed who she became and the actions she took as a result of those experiences. When we begin to see the joy in every experience we have, life looks brighter. We literarily feel lighter and even look more beautiful. There is a glow about us and we can achieve more. It does not mean the challenges fade away, but our joyful, positive outlook makes all the difference.

My last words will be, that being a busy working mum is one of the toughest jobs anyone can have. It is exhausting, scary and filled with momentary uncertainties. However, we can turn it into an exciting adventure by looking for the joy in every experience, embracing those experiences, appreciating the seasons of our lives, learning the lessons they bring and employing those lessons in future seasons as they unfold.

In my opinion, the toughest job can become the easiest by just taking things in their stride and employing these nuggets. They have been working for me and I trust they will work for you too.

ABOUT THE AUTHOR

Adeola is a passionate lover of life, nature and people. She expresses this passion in everyday life as a mum, an entrepreneur and a friend. She loves children and sees every child as a gift to our world. She draws strength and inspiration from her Faith. Her mantra in life is "...loving God includes loving people" 1John 4:21

Ebun Bilankulu- Breaking Free From Expectation And Looking Forward

"The best way to insure you achieve the greatest satisfaction out of life is to behave intentionally."

— *Deborah Day*

To many men and women alike, greatness or success is measured in tangible things and accomplishments in the form of earnings, properties owned, type or number of cars personally owned and so on. To others greatness is a measure of success in their chosen fields or their calling, as my Christian brethren would say. While for some, it is the amount of influence or power they hold and the degree of respect they command. Greatness for some can also be a combination of all the above in varying degrees.

We all want to be happy doing something that gets us some form of recognition or accolade and enables us to achieve set goals or ideals. "What makes you happy?" is my question to everyone What would you still love to do if money was not an issue, or time was not a constraint? What brings out the passion in you? It might not be something celebrated or lauded by society or even by family or friends, it might not be monetary or understood by people around you, but you owe it to yourself to be objective in your thinking, planning and charting out your path, and not comparing your life to other people.

I considered my life to be perfect as a single female. I was in a very good place, full of energy, ridiculously happy in my skin and with myself, setting goals and achieving them, loving the Lord and giving of my time to the church as a worker. Not giving much thought to marriage or children - except when I had to invent some super boyfriend to field questions about when I was likely to settle down and bear some children. This was usually over the phone to my well-meaning and very concerned family members. I was also very career minded and had this grand plan of doing a lot of professional things in my work life. According to some, by 'Naija' (fond name for my motherland) standards, I was fast approaching my 'best by date', not that I was too concerned. You see, I fell into a strange group of women that didn't mind being everybody's favourite Aunty with too many cats and no kids of her own. What I had learnt and seen of marriages growing up and as an adult was more negative, and I felt wasn't worth the trouble. I didn't have any rose-tinted lenses with which to view married life but I still had hope and expectations when I finally did get married, some of them I never realized were buried deep in my subconscious.

I remember the Preacher at our wedding saying, 'marriage is the only course in life that you get your certificate before you do the work' followed by, 'getting married is the easy bit, staying married is a different kettle of fish'. I honestly thought to myself, 'no way preacher man, that doesn't apply to us. You see me and this fine God loving brother here, we love each other sooooo much, we've got each other's backs, we are for keeps, No hard work for us to keep this marriage going, it's going to be a smooth journey as we grow from strength to strength and help each other along the way with Jesus at the centre of it all'.

Famous last words! Only a few weeks into this marriage showed me very quickly that the preacher man was right in so many respects. A union of two broken people from different backgrounds with different ideas of what's normal and what's not, is a recipe for disaster. I remembered my Mum always saying, "two wrongs will never make a right", every time I fought my husband but it took a lot of praying, soul searching, desiring peace and listening to Joyce Meyer to get the right balance of fighting fair and not ripping into the man I love and married even when I felt justified to do so. My husband and I were quite similar in that each of us wanted to have our way and I genuinely believed I always had the right solution to our problems. He just refused to toe the line.

We had our children quite early in the marriage, so we didn't have the leisure of spending much time together as a couple. Having children in our mix put a lot more pressure on our weaknesses and increased the things we fought about. Finances and priorities were big on our issues list. The main problem was how we communicated with each other about identifying and resolving issues. I had this terrible habit of listing all my husband's failings anytime we fought. I even prided myself on having an elephant's memory with regards to his transgressions since we got married, until he asked me why I never remembered the good things he did. That troubled me, I had to step out of being judge, jury and hangman of this man and let issues that are past and dealt with, stay in the past. It wasn't easy and I must confess I still have to bite my lips at times to stop myself starting some diatribe over some issue of yester years. In all honesty it is getting easier.

It is very easy to start losing the sense of being an individual when children come into the picture. As a mum, I have found it is almost a forgone conclusion that when you have a child, the momentum or even the trajectory of your career will change. I found out work and career did not have my 100% dedication and focus anymore. For a long time, I did not understand the struggles I had about returning to work full time, as I also struggled with staying at home as a housewife, stay home mum.

Mummy! Mummy!! Mummy!!!

When you feel like you've lost something of yourself.

And your time is not your own anymore.

When you become everybody's going to person.

Sometimes you get overwhelmed.,

My children mean so much to me, but frankly they can be EXHAUSTING! Just looking at them run around can be draining at times. But looking at their cheeky innocent faces means I can never be entirely selfish again (I can't believe it myself sometimes, the complete about turn from being a focused career minded individual to becoming a centered family person). I have to carefully consider the effects of my choices as a wife and a working woman versus a modern woman and career woman. So at least for now, I have laid to rest some grand plans I had for the future.

Like a wise man recently told me, 'the choices we make, come with both expected consequences and unexpected consequences'. Life can also deal out some interesting cards in unexpected places and unexpected ways - sickness, disability, loss, deception and more. We have had some serious challenges in our lives together, some self-inflicted, some just our share of life's many twists and turns. There are times you will need to be honest about what your relationship and children mean to you.

You also need to be open to change. Being a wife and a mum for me involves a lot of giving, of my time, my emotions, my peace of mind and at times I need something for me, so for that period I do an activity just for me and about me, like going to a dance class or taking a very long walk. Stepping out of the daily grind, I find myself in the things which remind me of a less involved time; reading a book, listening to music, praying and getting away for a short while to catch my breath and regroup.

Eight years on and still counting, my husband and I are still learning what makes each other tick, having decided that we are sticking together like a snail and its shell. At the start of this journey, me saying 'I love you' to my husband meant, you make me feel so good, treating me like a princess and all, I feel all fuzzy and weak kneed when you smile at me'. Now when we say 'I love you', it means despite our shortcomings, faults and failures, we are committed to staying together and growing together.

While the giddy heights of young love is exciting, the roots are quite shallow. Courting singles and newlyweds are usually on their best behaviour. In marriage, we get to see each other at our worst, good, bad and downright ugly. It is very important to learn your spouse's love language and quit comparing them to some other person or comparing your achievements with other couples, it only brings about frustration and misplaced anger; plus you don't have a clue as to what might be going on behind closed doors. So, my sisters, step out into reality, your reality. Don't be carried away by the Hollywood definition of what true love entails or what a modern-day woman should be like. That set me free to enjoy and celebrate the little, seemingly mundane aspects of marriage and children. While I am not the boss of some global corporation or even a local one for that matter, I am learning to celebrate my achievements as a person, though they don't exactly line up with the dreams and ambitions of my nineteen-year-old self.

I know I am my own worst critic, but I can be very generous in being a source of comfort when other people talk about their failings and shortcomings, perceived or real. I have decided, that on this wonderful journey of my life, not only will I be less hard on myself when I am not where I desire to be or when I act out of character, but I will also hold on to courage to start again whenever I fall short.

Life is a gift, and even in the midst of working, sacrificing and toiling to get ahead, supporting our families or whatever it is we are doing as women; we need to take time to relax, regroup and relate. I end with this, stepping out and releasing your inner greatness is relative to you and your circumstances. For some it is about doing something exceptional or making a career or business related decisions, for me it is about being an effective, happy, well-rounded wife, mother and individual. Being successful for me is not necessarily about making as much money as I can, living in the lap of luxury or climbing to the very top of a career ladder. I have decided what is important to me and where my greatness lies. You need to decide for yourself what is important to you as a person and do all you can to be the best in achieving that role. God bless.

ABOUT THE AUTHOR

Ebun - Wife, Mother and generally 'our girl Friday' on the home front; taking into account the multiple roles I get to play as a Mum, for which I have had no formal training, hence no qualification. I have received and continue to receive training from the University of Life helped on my way by the word of God. I have an eclectic work life and have dabbled in everything from the sciences, to retail, to administration, to care! I have been blessed enough to interact with a lot of women from various walks of life who are on the same quest of being the perfect Mum, as well as others who feel they have found the winning combination to be a woman with a balanced life. I see myself first and foremost as a Wife and Mother…my career or lack of it is secondary in my life.

Ibukunoluwa E. Ogunbola (aka Ibikay) – Finding Me After The Storm

"Efforts and courage are not enough without purpose and direction" - John F. Kennedy

In the beginning

Hi there, my name is IBUKUNOLUWA OGUNBOLA, I am a mother of two handsome and bubbly boys, a graduate of Ambrose Alli university with a degree in business administration and then some other certificates in catering. Event decoration, broadcast journalism and presentation. Before you go wondering what this has to do with anything, let me take you back to who I was before ever becoming a mum.

I am the first of five children to REV MK OGUNBOLA, a clergyman, my arrival into the family was received with great joy, at the time my mum was working, so my father took care of me. I am told I was a very quiet child and did not give my dad any trouble. My father loves music and always played for me. I am sure that was where I got so musically inclined, which by the way, is just one of my many gifts.

Aside from loving music so much, I found out I could sing well without any struggle, this made me join the choir at the age of eight. Singing for me was heaven, from there on, I began playing the drums as well as the bass guitar and became the first girl in my neighborhood to play the drum set. At the time, life was just sweet.

I had always been on the big side and those days people used to call my mother and me sisters, I believe this must have given my parents concern because most people addressed me like an older person, I began getting offers for a relationship from men way older than I was. I remember vividly my first marriage proposal; it was at the age of eleven. The second was at the age of fourteen. While all these where happening, my parents tried hard as they could to shield me from these wolves in men's skin.

STEP OUT

Those years girls were told if they ever allowed a man to touch them they would get pregnant. That trick worked for me, because I did not want to become pregnant out of wedlock, not with stories I heard of those who did, and the number of people who came for counseling with my parents.

These stories later informed my desire to have the best of marriages, and even become a counselor so I could help those who experience challenges in their relationships. These were the dreams I had, and it drove me to read books on relationships. Love songs were my second best. I was not allowed to read circular novels, so I was stuck with mystery novels. In all of this, my mum was more of a Margaret Thatcher to me when it came to advising on relationship issues. Her concern was that I never lose my virginity before marriage, so I will say I had very little knowledge on such matters, most of the talks I got were more like when Moses was giving the Israelites the Ten Commandments, it was a list of 'thou shall not'. As a child, I was a very fearful person, I had some experiences that led to that.

When I was five years old, I was almost raped by a family friend's son. Later during my primary education; this senior found pleasure in bulling me for no apparent reason. Those days, the fear I harboured in my heart was so much it began to affect my studies. Thank God for my teacher who was observant, hence taking it upon herself to find out what the issue was and saw to it that it was resolved. But it did not end there. The school organised an excursion for us students to learn more about computers by taking us to a computer company called Sigma House. We had the pleasure of sitting in front of a computer, inputting our names and having the computer interact with us. I was among the students chosen to do this and the computer asked me my name which I inputed, the next question it asked was if I believed in stars, which I answered NO, it then went on to tell me that if I did, I was going to die by the age of thirty-four. I did not tell my parents about this, but kept it in my heart and began living in fear.

Life as a mum

Fast forward some years later. I was now a full grown woman with desires and emotions which needed expression. I did mention earlier that my dad is a minister. The church I attended had those from the east as the majority. It didn't come as a surprise when I brought one of them home as my choice for marriage. My father asked me a couple of times if I was sure of my decision? I maintained my answer after going to pray about it as instructed. For me growing up I had seen how the Igbo men around took care of their wives and I wanted to experience such care and affection, but that did not come to be. It was almost as if that which I feared, was what happened to me. Before leaving my parents, my father told me then that I should know that if I left I could not return, as if he saw trouble coming. His words later haunted me as matters went from bad to worse.

STEP OUT

We got married and the day was eventful. I was so excited, even the rain that fell massively on that day could not dampen my mood, for me that day was the best day of my life and I was going to be given the license to do 'bad things'.

Our love journey started and we were inseparable. Love was sweet. Thanks to my observant husband who noticed some substance emitting from my breast, we went for a check up with the family doctor. The results of the test showed I had a hormonal imbalance, and would not have been able to have children. We began treatment and I prayed seriously the treatment would work. I got myself a book titled 'Super Natural Childbirth", read it through, and prayed the prayers, God heard us and I became pregnant with our first son. My joy knew no bounds. Hhis arrival was, and is still, a miracle I can't describe. Things were a bit tight for us at the time. I remember many times I didn't have money to go for pre-natal. Sometimes I didn't even have food to eat. I could not tell my parents, because I believed it was not proper. I did not want to belittle my husband before them, I loved him so much and saw that challenge then as just a little experience we will surpass. Overcome them we did and I had our baby safely without difficulty.

Our son grew to be so beautiful; you would think he was a girl child. I settled into motherhood and life as a wife and mother started.

As a busy working mum

I had always wanted to own my business. After secondary school my mum enrolled me at a catering school, where I learned making cakes and other beautiful things. Later on I went to learn how to make hats, as well as events management, because I was just crazy about crafts. Armed with all this training I was ready to begin my catering empire. I got a place with the help of my mum, then started, it was not easy. I was not making sales and soon packed up. I became a full-time mum, although thanks to my mother, I was still getting some cakes and catering jobs which fetched me a little money from time to time. All through this time, I was too scared to look for a job because I felt since I had a third class I would not be taken seriously.

As a man thinketh so he is, this is indeed true. Three years passed and I was still trying for a job. Whenever I looked at job adverts, I would tell myself I did not have what it took to apply for the job. I did not know my self esteem had begun to dwindle. I plunged into housework with a passion that could only emanate from someone seriously in love. I trusted my husband completely, and decided since I could not get a job, I will do my best as a housewife and help around the home as best as I could, so he would not have to worry too much. I did all the laundry, I even learnt how to put on the generator and do minor repairs like changing plugs. In short all the handy jobs around the house. I did them all, because his job did not allow for him to be around much. 5 am he was out, and most times midnight, or even later when he would return.

I worried a lot then and could only pray for God's protection upon his life. I polished his shoes, picked out his outfit for the next day and ensured his meals were ready with the little we had then. Thank God for mothers, mine was always sending things, and this helped us greatly. All these activities, though tasking, were fun to me at the time because I just loved my man, and wanted to make him happy. Then we were still very much great friends and whenever he returned I had the gist of how my day went with him and we will laugh and make love and just enjoy each other's company. For me he was the most caring husband in the world. He would talk about how I could turn my business into something really big, and we would talk and talk for hours. All seemed okay until he began coming home later and later. One day he left for work and did not return until after three days, it was then I began to take note of the cracks in our relationship and had this gut feeling that all was not well.

Anger, frustrations, stress.

The first time I noticed things were off in our relationship was when my son was just three months old. That day my landlord's son, who happened to be a very good friend, came visiting. After we had exchanged pleasantries, he told me what he was about to tell me was just for me to check for myself to be sure I was doing all I could to keep my home intact. I beckoned him to go ahead with what he had to say and what he said nearly shattered my world. At some times in my pregnancy, I had to leave home. He told me at such times my husband had brought someone home to spend the night. I defended my husband there and then, and told him he must have been mistaken. As soon as my hubby came home that night I relayed the discussion, and even went ahead to tell him how I told the guy he must have been mistaken. Of course his response was I should not listen to such people, as they are only jealous of our relationship, and that he could never do such. I believed him.

A lot changed after that. Suddenly a man, who at one time I could play with his phone, make phone calls with his airtime, could no longer leave his phone idle. If he is at Jericho when it rings, he will fly down from Jerusalem with speed to pick it up. He would no longer take calls when I was there. Keeping late nights became a routine. He blocked me from his page on Facebook, and at one point when I had the opportunity to handle his phone, I discovered there was no single picture of myself there. Ladies were always calling, and suddenly he became personal chauffeur to some of them. I was gradually losing my friend and confidant. Suddenly I became too fat for him and he would compare me to the ladies he worked with at the bank. We quarrelled and quarrelled. Going out with me became non-existent; there was always an excuse for it not being possible.

Earlier in our marriage having sex was not an issue, it was steady between us, but as soon as I was pregnant he told me it was best to avoid it because he did not want it to disfigure the head of the baby. Since he was a graduate of Biochemistry, I believed he knew what he was talking about. Shortly after that sex reduced to once a month if at all. I complained and I was told it's not food. Later I was advised by him to do surgery to lose weight. I cried and prayed but nothing happened. He said such negative things to me, talked down to me before family and friends.

At some point, he got physical. One of those days after slapping me thrice and telling how much he hated me and would divorce me, I foolishly went to the kitchen and brought him a knife to finish the job. At the instant, I was just tired and wanted to be done with it.

I did say I learnt a lot of crafts, but by this time, I found out I could not do most of them. I had stopped believing in myself, I saw myself as a good for nothing person, lost touch with all my abilities. I had heard him say so many negative things to me and about me, I don't know when I believed them and began to see myself as being incapable of any form of success.

My light bulb moment

Living with this kind of mind set made me look older. I cried a lot those times and always prayed never to meet friends, because I could not bear to have them see me the way I was. But I was too afraid to do something about my situation. I believed I could not amount to anything without him.

STEP OUT

Thank God for the Word, and countless friends raising me up in prayer. The more I read the Word and listened to music that spoke the word into my life, the more I began to realize I could do better and should never settle for less. I found out I needed to stand up for myself. A time came when he left as he always did. I decided it was time to take care of me. I had to stand up to him for the first time. Though it led to my having to leave, I decided there and then to begin to recover all I had lost.

I went back to school and got a certificate in Broadcast Journalism, certificate in Customer Care as well as a certificate in Presentation from the prestigious Federal Radio Corporation of Nigeria Training School. These certificates helped me get my present job as a presenter on a Radio show titled Sharing life issues with ChazB. My dream to become a counsellor came true, and gradually all my gifts began to return. Now I am a more fulfilled mum, living the life I have always wanted to live and seeing even greater opportunities ahead.

What am I trying to say? If I could get a second chance at life, so can you. It's time to STEP OUT, yeah most times the fear of the unknown can be crippling, but it is way better than remaining in one spot and not making progress. I am out and it has been a wonderful experience so far, I look forward to seeing you at the top.

ABOUT THE AUTHOR

Ibukun Ogunbola popularly known as ibikay the queen of voice, is a presenter, music minister, a relationship coach and marriage counsellor, helping people find hope in the toughest of circumstances, a co-host on Sharing Life Issues with ChazB. She is a happily married mother of two boys, Gideon and Stanley.

Part Two:
Forge Ahead

Morenike Asaju-The Place

"You were put on this earth to achieve your greatest self, to live out your purpose, and to do it courageously."
— Steve Maraboli

I am a Christian, a mother of three beautiful children. I am a certified chartered accountant. I run a logistics business with my husband of over ten years and I work full-time with a top tier leading law firm in Lagos, Nigeria.

STEP OUT

I believe that we were all created for a purpose, we were not just created to exist but to live life to its fullest, to live a life of value where generations call you blessed.

How it all started

I met my husband almost ten years before we got married. He was my friend and though he now tells me that he knew then he wanted to marry me, he did not say anything for fear of scaring me away as he is a bit older than I am. He waited patiently for me to complete my education and finish my National Youth Service Corps (NYSC). The NYSC is a program set up by the Nigerian government to involve the country's graduates in the development of the country. This is known as national service year program – and a condition for employment in my country. When I completed my NYSC program he came to my father's house to congratulate me and proceeded to inform me of his desire to marry me. We had known each other a long time but I still took a couple of months to be totally sure before I gave my response.

However, less than three months after our Introduction - In the Yoruba culture, an "Introduction" Ceremony is held so both families can meet officially. The idea behind this is to introduce key members of both families so they know their son or daughter's new relatives. It's usually a small affair, but these days, it's like a mini traditional wedding ceremony – I had to travel to the UK for further education. This was also less than six months to the traditional wedding (Engagement) and White wedding ceremonies.

Due to the long distance between my fiancé and me, there was a bit of friction while I travelled to study in the UK. This was mainly due to communication issues. I remember one time it got so bad that I called off the entire wedding. My mother intervened and talked some sense back into both our heads and plans recommenced.

I came back to Nigeria less than a week before my Court wedding (in Nigeria the wedding involves up to four different ceremonies!). I got married in Court on Valentine's Day 2007 and had my Traditional Marriage and White (Church) wedding the weekend following. It was beautiful. I had not finished my course of study so I had only one month before I returned to the UK. We maximized it.

Life as a mom

I returned to the UK as scheduled and a couple of weeks later, I found out I was pregnant (in my head I was like, is that how folks get pregnant? Lol!). I probably did the test up to four times before it sank in it was positive. My mum asked me to visit the GP and I was visibly surprised when he asked me what I planned to do with the pregnancy. I told him, keep it of course!

It was a tough period for me. The pregnancy did not give me issues at all but I was a student in a foreign country, working part time to get some experience, had to maintain my relationship with my husband from over the seas as we say and I was pregnant. I was juggling many balls. Many thanks to my mum and a big sister who supported me, as my husband had not joined me then.

I gave birth to my firstborn – a son – and I could not have been happier. The support from my mother cannot be measured for words. My husband arrived the UK about ten days after our son's birth. It was a wonderful re-union. I finished my course and headed back to Nigeria where I had two more children – girls, then got a lovely but demanding job in a top tier legal firm in Nigeria. Then the fun began!

As a busy working mom

With my high stress job, three super hyperactive children and a husband and business, plus I were a leader in my local assembly, I was juggling too many balls.

Eventually, these made me inconsistent, not very reliable and I broke down often, or dropped one or two and sometimes all of the balls on many occasions. I felt guilty for failing in my Christian duties, or my family – my husband had a very time-demanding job, so the family never saw him much as we wanted to. The pressure was on me to make up for both of us.

How things changed

Everything seemed not to work as I was always stressed, frequently short with the children, feeling guilty about it afterwards, not having a life for myself. One day, I just stopped. I took a step back and made some key realizations:

- I was not enjoying my life
- I could not do the things I wanted to do
- I cannot do everything
- I had lost my peace
- My marriage was suffering
- I was just always tired
- I needed a good plan in place to handle it all

So, I did the following:

- I got help – I got a live-in nanny to help with the children and do some light chores like loading the washing machine, and clean the house etc.
- I resigned from my roles which I honestly knew I could not handle with my calendar and took up another less demanding role.
- I found a way to leave the office on time – no unnecessary overtime.
- I got a hobby. Something I did just for the fun of it.

- I found a way to get some me time. Just me, no children, no husband, no chores, just me. To think, pray, plan or just read or be by myself. Whatever I needed. Sometimes, I just stayed back an extra hour at the office after closing, and sometimes I do it first thing in the morning or wake up a little earlier.

- Get a mentor or two. Someone has done whatever it is you are trying to do. Leverage on that. Their advice can prove to be invaluable.

Key learning

I am still learning as I continue this journey but below are some of the things I have learnt and which has helped me so far:

- You have to know yourself and be true to yourself.

- Be willing to ask for help. There is no shame in that. I ask my husband to help with the ironing. It is the one chore I do not like doing and the one he loves doing. So that worked out well for me.

- As a spin off from 2. above, do not be house-proud as my mum would always tell me. It simply means attentive to, or preoccupied with, the care and appearance of one's home. Do not be too overly focused on keeping every area of your house spick and span to the detriment of other more important things i.e. your health. If you are genuinely tired and unable to sweep the house, heaven will not fall but if you like me have the occasional OCD – Obsessive Compulsive Disorder – like Monk and cannot sit down until every looks at least presentable in your home, then get help. Get a cleaner come in a couple of days a week if you can afford it or any other option you can come up with.

- Sometimes you have to take things one at a time. You may not be able to do it all at once. Do not feel bad. Take your time and like the Scriptures say "this one thing I do… Philippians 3:13b."

- Continue to find ways to develop yourself. By undergoing training or simply reading books. This will not only stretch your mind, it will enlarge your capacity to think more, do more and eventually, be more. *"Enlarge the place of thy tent, and let them stretch forth the curtains of thine habitations; spare not, lengthen thy cords, and strengthen thy stakes* Isaiah 54:2".

My pastor used to say, 'you are only becoming what you are already becoming'. This simply meant that you are going to be who you prepare and plan to be and if you do not plan and prepare, you are also becoming that! A good example is what I and my friends who went evangelizing together used to encourage some friends I met when I was at the polytechnic, they felt they were older and couldn't go to school. We encouraged them to go back to school as it took four years to complete their university education on average. They were 26 then. We explained that the choice was theirs, they would still be 30years in four years, the only change was if they were going to be 30year old graduates with better prospects and opportunities or they were going to be 30 years old non-graduates still living life as they were.

- On your journey through it all, help people along the way. No matter how you feel about not having enough, someone else has even less. Make an impact on your way up or as Wilson Mizner said 'Be nice to people on your way up because you'll meet them on your way down'. You can always do something, give a gift, offer encouragement or candid advice, pray, laugh or cry with them. It makes a difference believe me. Life is not all about you and you do not have to make money out of everything! Some things can take you farther than money can. My father taught me that not so much in words as in deed. In all you do, find a way to leave a positive imprint. Like Maya Angelou said, "I've learned that people will forget what you said, people will forget what you did, but people will never forget how you made them feel." Do all you can get so that when you leave this earth, generations will call you blessed because you will have left a lasting legacy.

STEP OUT

- Make time to have face time with your children daily as much as you can. Give hugs and kisses frequently. Know what is going on with them, who their friends are, what new interests they have and any issues they may have going on. You will be pleasantly surprised. Do not be too busy providing for them and not have time for them. "Train up a child in the way he should go: and when he is old, he will not depart from it Proverbs 22:6"

- Leverage on your faith. "For we have not a high priest which cannot be touched with the feeling of our infirmities Hebrews 4:15", "I can do all things through Christ who strengthens me. Philippians 4:13".

- Treat others the same way you would like to be treated. It does not matter how you are treated, always walk in love. Be the kind of person you would like others to see and respect. Remember, people are moved more by what you do than what you say.

- Maximize the power of synergy. Two are better than one. Pray together with your spouse. Scriptures say, one will chase a thousand, two will put ten thousand to flight and a threefold cord is not easily broken when God is in the picture.

Advice/tips/shortcuts

- Ensure you have a solid system of communication in place with your spouse. In my home, we use a sandwich system. We sandwich every critique with praise. Honest praise. We correct in love. No foul language. Remember that "A gentle answer makes anger disappear, but a rough answer makes it grow. Proverbs 15:1".

- Have fun! Alone, with your spouse, with your family and friends, don't be too busy for rest and play "…but in the living God, who giveth us richly all things to enjoy; 1 Timothy 6:17"

- Take care of your body. Your health is very important. You cannot be on this earth without a body. It is your permit to be here on earth legally; else you become a demon which is why we can cast them out. Have annual checkups, exercise regularly, eat healthily and maintain a healthy BMI.

- Teach your children the foundations they need to have, to respect all people, how to handle money, family, faith, responsibility and being honest regardless.

- Learn about money management and investment. Work on passive income that you do not have to work for actively.

Today, Tomorrow, The Place

I am currently learning and training for a new skill. Something that would not only make me better and give me a hobby but is a potential source of income for me. I am also working on completing a couple of professional examinations in my chosen field that would not only improve me but also allow me to become a consultant in that field. I can see the future and as one of my pastors would say 'I need shades cos it's so bright'

I honestly cannot say I have reached where I would like to be, and where I know God is taking me to but I take pleasure in the journey.

I have learnt in my short stay on planet earth that nothing just happens. There is always a reason and a cause and effect. So, I make sure I do my part and after I have done all I know to do, I do as Joyce Meyer says *"Enjoy where you are on the way to where you are going to"*.

ABOUT THE AUTHOR

Morenike is a working mother of three beautiful children who works with a top tier leading law firm in Nigeria. She also runs a logistics business with her husband of over ten years. Morenike believes that we were all created for a purpose, we were not just created to exist but to live life to its fullest, to live a life of value where generations will call you blessed. Morenike is a chartered accountant and she holds a degree from the Oxford Brookes University in Applied Accounting.

ADETOLA OGBEBOR- LIFE IS NOT A DRESS REHEARSAL

"You weren't born just to live a life and to die; you were born to accomplish something specifically. Matter of fact, success is making it to the end of your purpose; that is a success... Success is not just existing. Success is making it to the end of why you were born" - Myles Munroe

So, like everyone who might be reading this right now, I was born into this world. And like we all have dreams to be this or that when we grow up, and desires to achieve several things, I had and still have mine too.

STEP OUT

From quite a comfortable background, my parents tried to give me their best or should I say equip me with the necessary basic ingredients for life. I went to school and of course got a daily and weekly dose of my dad's tutoring and modelling, which has been a foundation and propellant for my drive in life.

Just like every lady, I had dreams of being married and having a Godly family, (Husband and children) be wealthy, living in a beautiful house, working in a world class organisation, being a renowned public speaker, a prolific writer, and yet training others to succeed in their endeavors.

So those were the goals before me that I needed to work at achieving. But then, I realized it is not just about having beautiful dreams and goals, it is not even sufficient to think positively about your life, nothing happens by doing nothing about it. It is not okay just to have aspirations; I have got to push those goals into reality. If wishes could come true, I guess we would all be living our best of lives as we 'wish' it. But, the tests of life come to each of us at different times and unfortunately, we do not even have the opportunity or get the chance to pick what comes to us.

I always wanted to work in a global organisation with well laid out structures and system, a fantastic career path with all the juicy allowances. But that only existed in my imagination; the job I got was with more of a 'third world' organisation. Nonetheless, I took it and gave it my best shot, because I believe whatever one is doing now, is a stepping-stone or leverage to the next desired level and anyways no knowledge or skill is ever lost. It would always be useful sometime in the future.

I did not tell myself I had to be stuck in the job forever, because that is what I have got. I was always questioning myself, thinking and wondering that in about fifteen years down the line, After I have climbed to the peak of this career I am doing right now, would I be fulfilled? Would I be content? Or would I be a highly placed dissatisfied entity? Pause and think about this for a minute because ultimately, we determine our outcome in life by ourselves. Whatever decision we take or do not take will give birth to our future. Our future is just a multiplication of all the things we are doing or we are not doing now.

So, I kept discovering myself, learning and learning, un-learning and re-learning; because an individual that does not take time to access information is already deformed mentally. I took courses that I felt spoke to my inner being. Your inner being is the core of your existence, the one who can gauge whether you are doing what you ought to be doing or not. The person who gets satisfied or dissatisfied at the end of the day. The one who feels accomplished and fulfilled or not. That is where your purpose is rooted. That you have a good job and you can pay the bills does not necessarily mean that you are on point. That is not all there is to you, there has got to be more to a person than just living this way. I dare to say it is the lowest ebb of living. In fact, it is merely existing, not living. Mere existence is filling your life with activities which do not impact anybody but you. But living is the fulfilment of a defined agenda.

I wish I could say life has been all rosy and good. I wish I could just push a button and voila!!! All my dreams and wishes would be actualized in the twinkling of an eye. Wishes do not come to pass. Babe, you have got to exert pressure on yourself to bring out what you want to see on the outside. Any change you want to see starts with you. You have got to incubate it. It is your life. No conception, No delivery. It is as basic as that. The extra-ordinary life belongs to those who dare to give in the extra another would not put in. Life will give you what you demand of it, nothing will fall on you like ripe cherries off the tree.

Even as I sit to write this, it is past 11 pm and girl, I had a FULL day. Am I tired? Of course I am. I have to write this. Because what has to be done has to be done. Can I ask you a question, what matters most to you? What gives you fulfilment? What is your driving force? What are you living for?

As a woman, we get married and it seems there is so much on our plate than we bargained for. The plate gets fuller when the kids start arriving, and we are expected to keep everything under control. This minute you are happy, the next minute you are so overwhelmed, so angry at the enormity of work you must keep at. By that time some just resolve to be an 'MRS' and somebody's mummy and just continue with a dissatisfied busy life. But then, "busyness" is not necessarily achievement or accomplishment. Being "busy" is not even guaranteed success and may not make you fulfilled.

Dear woman, being busy is not a definition of you, that is not what you were created to do. You are a treasure, skillfully crafted for a specific purpose. You have so much to give your world. So much potential loaded in you with multitasking abilities. You are made of much more than you even think or know. All we need to do is take life one step at a time. Some skills and talent will not even be displayed until we stretch ourselves.

Through it all, I read a lot and inspire myself and keep 'Me' motivated by reading about people I admire and doing what I love to do. I tell myself I did not bring 'Me' to this world so there's got to be more to my existence. There must be a reason why I am here on this earth. I came to fulfil a mission. I am here on an assignment, which if I do not heed, may incapacitate some people because no man is an island. God put something in each of us for humanity. I must not allow procrastination to steal away my life. You were not designed to be a spectator.

There are gifts, skills, and talents that are on my inside that needs to be harnessed and cultivated to be used to make the world a better place. This propels me to keep pushing and not relenting. I make my today better than my yesterday. Today is all I have got. It does not matter what I did right or wrong yesterday, my today is what counts. That I am alive is an opportunity for better choices and actions. I must give my best today. Today is always another chance to begin again. When we lose sight of that, then we begin to get distracted by the things which do not make our existence worth it. And might I say, our existence is rooted in our maker. Nothing makes sense outside of Him. He is our source and sustenance.

Let me just quickly mention here that the associations you keep also determine to a large extent your outcome in life. Who do you hang out with? You can never rise beyond the friends you have. The closest company you keep will either move you closer to your dreams, or take you further away from them. Do you keep friends on purpose or you just move along with those that come your way? You have got to be deliberate about the people you associate with just as you are about your vision for your life. You must pursue friendships that align with your values to arrive at a worthwhile destination

Another vital principle of success for me is communication with God. As much as I can and as often as I can, I commune with God because he alone knows me inside –out. I do not even know me like He knows me because He created me. He put those desires and aspirations there. That means He is the one that can reveal me to me. Everyone can try to describe me to me, but God knows exactly who He made me be. One thing I have come to realize is that what you were fashioned for is even beyond you. There are several people that will

STEP OUT

be liberated just because you worked on an idea, you executed a project or you just followed an innate desire.

Life is not to be lived for one's self, that is being selfish. You must share your uniqueness with everyone you come in contact with in this life. Anything below this is short-changing the real you. Life is not a dress rehearsal; it is the real deal. It is a one-time offer, no second chance; you have got to use it well. Do not let the 'I will do it sometime in the future' eat away your life. Time waits for no one. It just keeps moving and moving and moving. Unfortunately, lost time is a part of your life that can never be recouped. All you need to do is to be determined to stretch!!! Nobody ever achieved anything without stretching and nobody ever died while stretching. To be the total package that you were born to be, you must be willing to go beyond your comfort zone and not just dance to the status quo music. The status quo region is already overcrowded, you must rise to be that woman who finds a way in all she is involved with and uses the challenges she encounters on a daily basis as a spring board to attain great height.

So, woman, you are one because you can handle so much, and the one who made you believes in whom he made. Live!!! Be determined. Do not give up on your dreams, embrace values and beliefs that would mold the future you want and be diligent about it. Nothing can replace diligence. It always produces. Push through, and dare to be the best version of you. Pay the price for the prize, Step Out and release your inner greatness.

ABOUT THE AUTHOR

Adetola Ogbebor is a Certified Life Coach who helps individuals and corporate entities maximise their potentials by harnessing the resources at their disposal. A self-motivated and detail oriented individual who loves to bring change and add strategic value to her immediate environment, and will stop at nothing to achieve the best in all she does. She is also a prolific writer and an ardent counsellor with a passion for people development and leadership enhancement. She is married and has two beautiful kids. She loves music and the colour - Blue!

Kelle Wares- Learning the Meaning of Serenity

"Not everybody can identify a purpose in life. But when you do, and when you pursue it, you will be living the kind of life you feel you were meant to live. And what's more, you will be happy."
- Steve Goodier

It became clear to me from as early as eight years old, that people can't be taken at their word, trusted or relied upon. Growing up it was just me, my little brother, and mum. It didn't take long to settle down as a family of three in our new home after my parent's divorce, in what now looking back was the best start in life a parent can ask for. Good old fashion village life style. The view from our front room window is still as beautiful and picturesque as the first day we moved in. Horses in the fields that go on for miles

On my eleventh birthday, my little sister came into the world, joining us. Now we were a family of four. I didn't have many friends growing up, never feeling I could trust many people. I did make some lifelong friends who I'm still very close with to this day. We aren't in each other pockets or see each other daily but we are always there for each other.

Fast forward a couple of years and I discover boys!! Fourteen years old I have my first boyfriend. First teenage love, so innocent and naïve. I lost my virginity with the father of my oldest son. This teenage love only lasted only a mere six months. Hey, I was fourteen years old what did I know about love, life, relationships, and I didn't have a clue the contraception pill wasn't foolproof.

Let alone Kelly proof. As it so became clear, nothing is Kelly proof, as you will see as you read on. I'm not complaining as my life may not have been easy or like most people's life, I would say it's been eventful and very colourful to say the least.

I was in a new relationship with my second son's father. My mum noticed I was piling on the weight quickly. So, my mum being as she is, I was up the doctors having tests and yes, they did a pregnancy test and it was negative!

STEP OUT

Three weeks before my fifteenth birthday I had my first positive pregnancy test and it came as a big shock!! Now this is where it gets a little bit complicated. Me being me, I don't do things by halves. So, I'm all happy and excited about having a baby. I'm at the baby clinic having my first scan for my due date and I'm told I'm further gone than first thought, so thinking I'm a few weeks more but no I'm 20 weeks pregnant, *20 weeks*, I was pregnant the whole time. The test was all wrong.

My world went into a crazy spin. I went home and I had to have one of the hardest conversation as a fifteen-year old girl could have. I had to explain to my current boyfriend that he isn't the father and I'm pregnant with my ex's child.

As selfish as this will sound, I was only with my boyfriend three moths at this point. I knew and didn't care who was the father was. This baby was mine, all mine. This was my first real chance of giving and receiving unconditional love. This was something I craved for so long. I always felt something was missing from my life, even though I was so young. The moment I found out I was pregnant, I felt complete like this was meant to be. I have never had a regret or felt I made a mistake becoming a teen mum.

I have been blessed to have a family that supported me, never judged me, or said I was too young to have a child. Well, they never said it to me. I already had a weekend job as a waitress at a pub in the next village. I saved all my money to spoil my child with the best of everything.

STEP OUT

The pleasure I got from shopping for my child was crazy, to this day nothing makes me happier than spoiling the people I love.

My mum informed the school I was attending and what a drama that caused. Meeting after meeting and governor after governor meetings. The governors decided that having a teenage pregnant girl in the school was not the image they wanted to portray to new parents and child attendees. So, for health and safety for myself and the students I could not stay at the school.

The plan was for me to go to the mother and baby unit in Bristol. The only problem was they couldn't take me at that point in time. They decided that home tutoring was the only option. Six hours a week and five subjects. I'd gone from doing an average of C grade and above in 12 GCSE to 5 GCSE equivalence. What a confidence boost that wasn't. Young, cut off from my daily routine of school and friends, not going to achieve the education I always thought I'd have. It felt like I was being written off all because I choose to have my son. That was a hard pill to swallow.

From Sept 1995 to March 1996 sat at home doing nothing much until my son popped out in January 1996. What an easy baby he was so good. I was so damn lucky. I started my home tutoring in March and everything had to be in and complete by end of June. I had to condense a year's work in a couple of months. I was feeling as though I was being set up to fail. I'm sure it's not how it was, it's just how I was feeling.

What made things worse was living in a village, the gossip was horrible. The things that were said about me and my mum. But I proved them all wrong, my son was never in care. I am a good mum not perfect, but my sons will always be my world and come first till the day I die.

My relationship with my mum became so close because of my sons, for that I am forever grateful.

She is my rock; my family is my whole world and that will never change. She has had my back from day one, kept me going through the dark days with my sons. Inspired me, built my self-esteem back up, help to believe I can be a good mum and made sure I remembered I am also Kelly too. Never shying away from telling me how it really is as a parent and being a single parent. The love and support I had daily from my mum and auntie, they helped me crush my self-doubts.

I have three empowering strong women in my life my nan RIP, my mum, and auntie. All completely different women and all brought something different to the table. Not one of them let me stay in my pity parties for long. As a parent, I'm pleased my sons grew up to have strong connections with them. The memories we all share and wisdom that will be passed down to the children, makes me proud.

At sixteen I got my first full time job. What rollercoaster

rides my work life has been over the years. Far too many long hours, working multiple jobs most of the time, minimum wage and living from pay check to pay check. I felt like I could never catch a break or get ahead financially.

I had a complicated pregnancy with my youngest son and in and out of the hospital from day one with him. This was a struggle for me balancing a new home, the poorly baby of 1 year old, 4year old starting school and a new part time mininimy wage job at my local shop in the village where we lived and all by the time I was 18 years old. That is a juggling act and a half to do. Once I got into the swing of things, learnt that I couldn't control everything especially when it came to kids. It didn't take long to realise just how happy and content I was with my little family and our life. We didn't have much but we never went without anything either.

After years of being the one who fought for everything, supported everyone in my family and taking care of my friends, I had become the go to person to solve life problems. Did I mind? No it gave me purpose, and I was proud that I could help make a difference in people's lives.

February 16th, 2010 my life would never be the same again. Everything I once knew and called my life was gone. I wasn't me anymore.

One moment, one action, one personal choice brought

STEP OUT

my world crashing down and changed my life forever. I was a shell of the woman I once was thanks to this situation. What was the situation that caused my life to spin out of control and effect my future forever…?

I was drugged and raped. Yep I said it aloud. You have no idea how hard and how long, it's taken me to admit this and accept it and say it aloud without shame and guilt. Yes, it was by someone I had met before and was introduced to them by someone I classed as a very good and close friend. So yes, I trusted this person.

It took me eighteen months to accept this had had happened to me. No, you never accept it, you learn to live with it. It's like losing someone close to you. You never get over it you learn to live day by day.

I spent so many months doing anything I could to block out the imagines that flash back at the worst times, certain smells can trigger me into a crazy bender of alcohol and drugs. There really is only so much you can do to block things out without the people you care about have had enough. Especially when no one knows what you're living inside your head every second every minute and every single day.

My oldest son was the worst effected by all this we clashed daily over my drinking. The states he found in me regularly. We would argue so often it was becoming a normal thing, then things just kept escalating, things were smashed often and we even got physical and fought. All I cared about was getting high and drinking myself stupid so I would pass out and not have to deal with things.

Avoidance was becoming second nature; my temper was at the boiling point all the time. I was angry, bitter, twisted. And at times I had no idea what was wrong with me, as I had suppressed it so well. Or so I thought. The reality was, I was broken in every way possible. Alcohol and drugs had been my best friends for so long to help me cope.

Let's be honest, I have no idea on how to deal with things in a positive way. My family wasn't talkers, often I was told to get it together and get on with my life as I'm screwing it up. I guess my family has a get on with things and move forward attitude. Easier said than done when they have no clue of what's going on.

While all this was happening, I had started a great job I loved. Perfect hours, dream company I wanted to excel in. You're thinking, something positive to focus on, because I know I did. I had a manager who can only be described as odd. Something was just off with him, from the way he looked to his personality.

I should of have trusted my gut instinct, this guy sexually assaulted me at work. Not once or twice, three times and had I not told my trainer who was in store for more one on one training. I believe he would still me doing this and to other women he works with.

STEP OUT

What a shambles the investigation was. The head office mishandled it from day one. They thought an apology would be ok and for me to continue working with him. I didn't think this was acceptable as I had heard rumours he done this before. This time I wasn't going to be quiet I can't risk him doing this to someone else. In my mind, I was concerned about was how far will he go where does he stop before its rape.

I got a solicitor and round Two began. Finally, a second person came forward and gave a statement of her experience, and it was the same as mine. Finally, I could breathe again. They listened and stepped up as a company and my second proudest achievement was standing up for myself and other women to stop him, but also taking on an international company and making them issue worldwide a handbook and complaints handbook so no one would ever have to go through the battles I went through.

Only took two and half years to do and once it was over I finally crumbled. I couldn't fight any more, all the last four years had drained me to a shell of women. I was severely depressed and suffered from anxiety. I was so ill, I was suicidal. I was broken and couldn't see a way out to fix myself. I believed everyone would be better off without the crazy mess of a person I had become.

Why am I still here? Honestly my biggest fear was the damage and pain it would cause my sons if they found my dead body.

And that is still is the only reason I get up and face my daily battles that still go on inside my head every single day.

The road to recovery is far from over and far from easy. This is something I have come to realise I will have to work on for the rest of my live.

Because of my illnesses I discovered network marketing and I thought this will be a piece of piss to do. I can't work retail stores due to my social anxiety but that didn't mean I couldn't work, right?

Wrong this profession, and yes, it's a profession, a new way of working and I believe it's a better way too. Is it easy? Hell no way, can you make fast money from day one? Don't be silly. It's like any career you train for, it takes time and you need to the skills to make you effective and most importantly you must have the right mindset. I have spent the last two years working on my mindset. Reading everything, watching videos, listening to podcasts. Which is all great, but until you step up and step out of your comfort zone, nothing changes nothing happens.

Without fail, daily I listen to Gabrielle Bernstein, Ray Higdon, Mel Robbins, Niyc Pigdeon, Eric Worre, Emma Privilege - a life couch I found on Facebook to help me. Without whom I wouldn't be where I am today.

Facing up to my fears, breaking down my walls, building my confidence and starting my own business has been positive, but hard, life changing experience. Do I struggle still? Yes daily, but now I have things in place. My daily routine helps build on my positive mind and actions are working. I have control over my life. My life doesn't run me into the ground. I'm living proof that when you can see this light at the end, you must keep the faith and believe the lessons you're learning will lead you to a better future. It led me here, to this moment in time, typing this with the hope that if my story helps, empower, inspire one person everything was worth it. After all this is my new beginning!!

ABOUT THE AUTHOR

Kelle Wares has gone from young teenager, to a kick ass teen single mother of her two sons. Who is now a thirty-something, embarking on a new mission - life after kids. She is entering a new phase of life and is determined to live it to the fullest and on her terms.

She is known to her family and friends as a straight talking, tell it like it is woman. For the first time, she is letting people in to her world and sharing her story to help empower women and just to let them know its OK to want it all, and we can have it all. We are not defined by our situations or society, but we are defined by our thoughts, the inner dialogue we tell ourselves daily. I am strong enough. I deserve it all. I will achieve it all.

Tutu Ademola (aka TU2) - An Enjoyable Challenge

"The purpose of life is to live it, to taste experience to the utmost, to reach out eagerly and without fear for newer and richer experience." — *Eleanor Roosevelt*

My name is Adetutu, popularly known as 'Tutu'. Friends from way back call me 'Tu Square' / 'Tu2', some even make it sound funky and they call me 'Tutsy', while the older folks call me 'Adetutu omo Oba' (child of a King), but in all I am a child of the Almighty God.

I am a Christian. Passionate about the things of God, blessed with four generations passing through my womb and a man not afraid of me achieving my God's given purpose. I have over 15 years experience working in the Financial Services industry, a passionate believer in a woman's ability to do Exploit, be a Solution provider, helping those around me to achieve the purpose and giving back to the Community.

I currently work as a Senior Consultant with one of the Financial Services providers in the UK and recently ventured into Real Estate, combining my experience in the Banking sector with Property Management and Investment. I'm loving every moment of it.

A working Mom - An Enjoyable Challenge

I had the luxury of being able to make my own decisions without having to constantly re-assess the impact on people around me. Of course this was before I became a Mom! Then, I think of buying the latest handbag in town and off I go!

The Babies, My Life, My Passion

When the babies started arriving, my priorities instantly changed. I have always been a career person, I quickly learnt how to have a family and work life balance. I made a DELIBERATE attempt to create time to spend with my family. The word 'deliberate' in caps, as it needed to be planned otherwise all other things over shadow those precious family times we need together. Children grow so quick and before you know it, they are no longer babies. My 1st son is taller than me now!

My focus now changed from 'me' to 'them'. Any decision comes with in-depth consideration of the impact of such decision on my children. No matter how juicy the offer looks, if it impacts my ability to fulfill my parental responsibilities as a Mom, I wouldn't accept it. The ability to make such choices now is because I stepped out of my comfort zone, identified my passion and took action.

After working about six years in the Banking sector in Nigeria, I decided to improve my career prospect and enrolled for an MBA in the UK. At the time I started the Program our 2nd son was barely six weeks old! One part of my heart kept saying, 'Tutu how on earth can you be starting a full-time education with a six weeks old baby'. I had the support of my wonderful family, God bless my dear Husband, Mum & Sister who were there to support me through this journey. It was indeed a big decision.

I started the course, met new friends from all over the world, settled in nicely but missing the family. Some days I get back from the Business School and I cry till I fall asleep wondering how I was going to cope. In those days, I so missed my Pounded Yam and Efo riro, Ewa Agonyin & Dodo and of course my favorite Ikokore Ijebu cooked with shawa fish. The African food was in limited supply then compared to what is available today hence it was quite expensive for my pocket and there was only a limited quantity I can bring when I go visiting.

But one thing I did was never to give up, I remained the focus, there was a Purpose for this, I had a Vision, I needed to find my Place and Position. When I look back, I am glad I stepped out of my comfort zone.

It's another big decision time

Fast forward to end of my Program, the Banking Sector was in crisis and going back to my previous role didn't quite work out as previously planned. I 'borrowed myself brain' as my 'Naija' people would say, we had to re-plan and that was where the journey began we decided to migrate to the UK.

Soon after I finished my MBA, I secured a job in the Financial Services sector here, I was alone with 2 children (we only had 2 then), I was yet to pass my driving test then (mind you it's not a luxury to drive a car here especially with kids and the unpredictable British weather!), there was no Uber in those days. I can write a whole book on passing a driving test, it's easier to pass if you have never driven before in a place like my dear home country. I had to first purge myself of all the bad driving habits.

It was a very cold morning during the Winter, the temperature was about -5°C, dropped off our 1st son in the before school club, his school was about 15 minutes walk from the house, then off to drop our 2nd son with the child minder, another 25 minutes walk from the school. I then noticed both of my hands were frozen even with winter gloves on. I couldn't push the stroller any more, a passer-by had to help me to the minder's house. I still think it was an angel who helped me that day. Later on that same day I decided that on my next test attempt I must pass and I refuse to be nervous anymore. Of course, I passed the next test and I then realized that if I didn't allow the nerve get the hold of me previously I would have probably passed on my 1st attempt. Lesson learnt!

Lines in pleasant places

Things started to fall in place, settled in the role but the job kept me in the office for very long hours and sometimes weekends. I didn't enjoy it. I couldn't dedicate time to the family. Oh I forgot to mention that my job involved constant communication with customers, so I had to quickly learn how to understand different accents, otherwise a customer might just get frustrated while I am trying to figure out what they were trying to say. I crossed that hurdle, got another better role and its been getting better ever since.

I never gave up, I was determined to add value to myself and be in control of my choices.

I knew there was a price I needed to pay, this wasn't going to happen over night, persistent and focus was the word. I knew where I was going, ignored the naysayers, identified my purpose, focused on my strength, had a road map for the vision and of course committed it in the hands of God.

My husband, jokingly always say this 'Tutu has it all planned out', 'she has programmed ten years of next steps and activity, you can't catch her unawares'. He is right! I focus on the goal, have a timeframe for the achievement, constant re-appraisal on my progress and put in more effort wherever I fall below expectations.

The journey now

I currently work full-time, my office is about 75 miles away from where I live. Approximately, that's about 4 hours return journey when I am not working from home. I also run a Property Management Business in addition to being a Mum of 4!

I guess you would wonder, how on earth does she manage to juggle all these responsibilities together. A popular saying that, been a Mum itself is a full-time job.

Although, being a busy working Mom comes with it's fun. Things like rushing out to attend an event and realising when I got to the venue I had a two different pair of shoes on, one was a black colored shoe and other was a red one, or realising I left the house with my flip flop on. But guess what, because I am a busy working Mom, I keep at least 2-3 pairs of shoes constantly in the car and sometimes I keep a spare handbag in the car as well.

Tips on how I get going

- Prioritize:

I have a 'to do' list. Only activities that add value makes it to that list.

- I cut off any excess 'baggage'. If a conversation/place is not worth my time, then I shouldn't be there

- Over the years I development myself. Constantly educating myself around my career path. When you are knowledgeable, you have the deciding power to make choices that would give the flexibility required to enable you to fulfill your parental responsibilities.

- I identified a Mentor who has walked each of the paths I am aiming for. My mentor is my 1st point of call when I need help to figure things out in the specific area he/she is mentoring me. I have three distinct mentors (Career, Business and Spiritual).

- I am an action taker. I identify what needs to be done and go for it.

- I deliberately create a family time. Set aside time to spend with my children.

- I buy in bulk, saving me constant shopping

- I use technology to make my life easier:

- You would never catch me roaming the whole

of 'Bull Ring' in Birmingham doing any form of shopping except it's just a day out to catch fun. Imagine, going to town shopping for four children! I go online, within a couple of minutes pick what I need, it gets delivered at home. The job was done! Time saved! More time to focus on other things.

- Automate all bill payments, set reminders to keep me on top of activities

Obviously, as a busy working Mom I see myself as a role model to my children and the younger generation around me. Keeping myself organized, showing them how to balance those responsibilities puts them in a better position in future to do far above what I have achieved.

On a final note, my advice is to keep learning, never give up, focus on the goal, cut off distractions, plan and re-plan until you get it right. If I can do it, you can do it too!

ABOUT THE AUTHOR

My name is Adetutu, popularly known as 'Tutu'. Friends from way back call me 'Tu Square' / 'Tu2', some even make it sound funky and call me 'Tutsy' but in all I am a child of Almighty God. I am a Christian. Passionate about the things of God, blessed with four generations passing through my womb and a man not afraid of me achieving God's given purpose. I have over fiteen years' experience working in the Financial Services industry, a passionate believer in a woman's ability to do, exploit, be a solution provider, and give back to the Community. I recently ventured into Real Estate, combining my experience in the Banking sector with Property investment. I love every moment of it.

Part Three:
Breaking The Rules

ADETOLA TY TAMUNOKUBIE- GRASS TO GRACE

"Knowing your life purpose is the first step toward living a truly conscious life. A life purpose provides us with a clear goal, a set finish line that you truly want to reach" –Simon Foster

I was born in Mushin, a suburb in Lagos State, on February 26, 1984. I am the last and only female child of three children. Growing up in Mushin was not rosy, but God brought me from the backside of life and truly I am convinced that God is the glory and the lifter of my head.

STEP OUT

My schooling is a mix of formal and informal education. But I will talk about the formal part here and mention the informal part in other parts of my story. I started primary school at age five, then moved to the north at nine and moved back to Lagos at ten. I completed my secondary education in 2000 and gained admission to Lagos state Polytechnic at nineteen. Surprisingly I enrolled for Chemical Engineering because I have always loved to be an entrepreneur. I had dreams of manufacturing household items, beverages and so on.

While I was a student, I still got involved in the business; I would buy clothes and jewelry from Yaba market and sell them to fellow students. The business helped me in taking care of my needs on campus. I could buy my handouts; even pay my school fees before my parents gave me money.

I learnt how to do business with my mum; while I was in secondary school I helped her sell at the shop after school and during the break I would also hawk matches, soap and other goods to raise funds to support my education.

Asides engineering and my dream to be a manufacturer, I also had a passion for media. At sixteen I had an idea to start an entertainment show. The idea tugged at my heart and I couldn't let go. Eventually, I contacted a TV presenter who gave me an idea of what it takes to produce a TV show; he also gave me contacts of few musicians. My brother and I contributed money and we shot a pilot copy of "Entertainment Extra TV show". I took it to a TV station but it was rejected.

Take Your Opportunity!

At age nineteen, I met the former marketing manager of a TV station, who said he tried to contact me but he couldn't because I didn't leave a number with him, so he asked if I could host his entertainment show. I accepted the offer and began working part-time for free.

After my OND (Ordinary National Diploma) I became fully employed as a presenter and reporter. Later on, I volunteered to work with the marketing dept. I worked 8 am – 6 pm, sometimes 12noon – 12 am or round the clock at Azhie communications, my industry demands that. In media, you have to be up-to-date. It demands spontaneity.

I decided to follow my passion since it was what I had always wanted. The pay was so small but I enjoyed what I was doing. I travelled every Friday from Lagos to Ogun state to host a show every for close to two years, then I went back for my HND (Higher National Diploma) part-time. So, I was working and schooling.

I left Ahizie Communications and moved to Maxima Productions, where I worked for close to three years. Working at Maxima Productions was an eye opener for me, I learnt a more excellent way of production and that was the turning point for me; I was transformed and I saw young people like myself doing great in their career.

Then I found it difficult to leave Maxima Productions even though I was certain about leaving. I always give my best wherever I work or in anything I get involved in. I owned my job and I gave my best with little or no supervision at Maxima. Finally, I resigned to start my own media outfit "Eltee Production Company".

But I did not start out just like that. I launched out with experience and knowledge of the industry.

Behind-the-Scenes of Eltee

I met my husband just before leaving Maxima Productions and he worked, prayed and planned with me. I thank God for a godly relationship.

My spouse and I started running Eltee Production Company. We started with a radio show then extended our production with a TV show, Entertainment Extra, which is running on eleven TV stations in Nigeria. We currently have two drama series, one parenting show and one entertainment show on TV and a radio sports show.

After we got married we encountered few challenges including financial challenges; our business was still at its baby stage. I got pregnant two months after our wedding, but I was told I had an Ectopic pregnancy. We took God's word and prayed about the condition. I was meant to undergo an operation but my baby went back into the womb before the proposed operation day and to God's glory, I gave birth to our first daughter, then it dawned on me that motherhood is a different ball game. I couldn't do all the things I was doing before she came; I would have to plan and consider her before I even thought of myself. Then the second child came, but in the midst of it all I still had time for my husband and kids, though it was not an easy one.

I would come back tired and sometimes when we were filming we came back later. At times, we came back the following morning and made it up to the children.

I am blessed to be married to a godly Christian husband. He is the best thing that ever happened to my business and career. He has helped me push my vision; he began this even before we got married.

As a busy working mum, I leverage my relationships and people around me. My mother helped out by taking care of the children, she did everything you can imagine. I am also blessed with a good mother-in-law. My in-laws stay about twenty-five minutes' drive from my house. Whenever I have a production or any other major engagement, I take my children my in-laws' house or my mother-in-law comes over to the house. My husband's siblings also come around and they have been a great help too.

I take my kids and maid to my mother -in-law or she comes over to my house.

Marriage and Family

We got married. And in all sincerity, after God, I owe my success to my husband and marriage. My marriage provided me with wonderful in-laws that I wouldn't trade for anything. My mum and maid always assisted too.

One day in church, someone alluded in passing that I didn't have time for my kids because, according to her, she did not see me carry them in church but I had to find out what works and what does not work. I believe in doing what I alone can or should do and then delegating housekeeping, laundry and other house chores. I take responsibility for my kids but I ensure that my vision, purpose, career and business are not contained because of parenting.

If you want to be successful and strike a balance, you must delegate. You can't be all over the place in town and at home, you alone shouldn't be the one who will take your kids to school, go to the office, cook for your family, attend to your husband, bath your kids and go to the market. In this regard, my mother and in-laws have been very helpful.

I help my kids with their homework and after school assignment and also visit their school often to find out how they are faring in school. I cook as much as I can and attend to my husband.

STEP OUT

I inculcated the right manners and godly living with my three-year old and two-year old daughters and taught them how to pray. In fact, they both take their prayer slot during the morning devotion. I take them out as many times I can; I watch TV with them and bond with them. I check their body parts and ask them questions about who did what and how their day went.

Initially, the driver took them to school with my mum or mother-in-law but later, I signed up for the school bus.

My husband and I had to resort to the school bus for our kids to ease the stress off us, my husband also insisted that I get a driver to be more effective and productive. I opposed it initially because I felt I could drive myself but he insisted, and that single decision helped balance my busy lifestyle. My job involves taking notes on the go; whenever an idea came to my mind I would always forget before I got to my destination. But after getting a driver, I began taking notes; I planned better, read, listened to a message while I am being driven. Going for meetings, marketing and communicating on transit became a whole lot easier.

Balancing motherhood and work also involves planning. Somethings I plan for family outings or even shopping for my children. You can't let these things stumble upon you. If you don't plan, you will be caught unawares, you will look back and discover that you left many important and necessary things undone. Life, work, clients and issues will fight for your attention, so plan and keep your family at heart.

My job involves taking notes on the go, ideas strike and how do I manage that? With the help of a driver I could catch up

PURPOSE, Vision, Career and Business

I am an associate member of APCON (Advertising Practitioners Council of Nigeria) and the social and welfare secretary of EMCOAN (Electronic Media and Content Owners Association of Nigeria).

Final words

You can't differentiate your success from your personality and character, before and after I got married, I had accepted my in-laws and we were on relating terms. I never knew they would be pivotal to me striking a balance as regards my work and career.

ABOUT THE AUTHOR

I am an exceptional media practitioner, marketing Specialist, movie/content producer and a fashion enthusiast. I have an undying passion to create standard and world-class contents and to revolutionize the Nigerian broadcast industry through outstanding contents.

Dr Mary Pellicer- From Doctor to Healer, My Journey of Discovery

When I was eight years old, my father moved our whole family to Rabat Morocco. He had taken a job as a physician for the Peace Corps for two years. In Morocco, I first heard my calling as a healer. To me, healer meant doctor because of my Dad.

To my very young, small town raised American sensibilities, Rabat was often a confusing jolt. I remember going to the market with our maid, Millie, and seeing beggars lined up along the winding paths, their pleading hands outstretched trying to catch our attention. I vividly remember one man with no legs; he moved his torso by walking on his hands. Another woman with no nose, just holes directly into her face, shocked me; I had no idea such deformities existed. Then there were the babies, little bundles slung on their mother's backs with matted eyes and runny noses, flies buzzing incessantly around their faces. My tender little heart went out to all of them and I yearned to help.

I knew my Dad helped sick people because that is what doctors do. After all, he was always there to take care of us when we were sick. I do not recall the precise moment I decided my life path, although in retrospect I think it was when touring a refugee camp and seeing all those sick babies swaddled on their mothers' backs. Whenever the precise moment, the result was I came home from Morocco determined to become a doctor. As a young child, I had committed to the journey of health, not only for myself but for those who had no one else to care for them.

The Path of Lifelong Learning

All through school, grade school, high school and into college I stayed on this path. I have always had a voracious appetite to learn and I excelled. I was especially fascinated by the science of all types, which led to some interesting episodes. For example, I may have dissected a few dead animals I found along the way including a poor unfortunate cat that accidentally froze to death. And then, there was the time I became intrigued with the possibilities for alternative protein sources. Most unjustly in my opinion, I got in quite a lot of trouble for putting earthworms in the chicken soup one evening while babysitting. My siblings, I'm afraid, had no understanding of my genius.

Through all the various ups and downs of my early life, my big goal, to be a doctor, was always there, shining as my beacon when the going got rough. Through high school and beyond, I struggled with depression and my magnificently wonderful husband was my rock of stability and support through medical school and residency.

After my family practice residency, we moved back to our hometown, I went to work for an organization that did migrant and community health. As a freshly fledged physician, I struggled to assist my patients. I began to realize the limitations of conventional medicine as I had been trained. Most of the patients I saw had chronic health issues: diabetes, asthma, heart disease, arthritis, depression, the list goes on. Often, they could not afford the medications I had been taught to prescribe. They struggled to make the changes necessary to help them manage their chronic illness, whether that was a diet change, stopping smoking, exercising more or changing other life patterns. Something didn't feel right and I grew increasingly frustrated as I tried to guide my patients toward improved health. I finally left the clinic and became the medical director of a healthy community program for a hospital system; we were exploring how best to do health in partnership with the community. I learned the vital importance of an accepting, supportive community when people are making life changes.

Children Are Such Amazing Teachers

By his time, I had two children of my own. I can tell you for sure that taking care of children is a lot easier when reading about it in textbooks than doing it up close and personal 24/7. After having my own, I seriously rethought a lot of the glib advice I had naively handed out to parents. Seriously, I didn't have a clue.

Our two incredibly wonderful boys have taught me so much, when things went well and even more so when there were problems. We dealt with our share of childhood illnesses and my first big lesson in the importance of eating a healthy diet came when we shifted how we fed them and watched the number of sick days drop significantly. I began to read all I could talk about nutrition and how it impacted health. This was an area that was not addressed in medical school, so I worked to play catch up. My husband, bless his heart, worked to keep me from being overzealous—we made a good team. I was learning to use nutrition to heal; he was keeping me grounded in reality.

The Downside of Pushing for Success

STEP OUT

As I continued my work for the hospital, I was helping develop new programs in our community I hoped would be more than mere band aids for health problems and would instead start to get to root causes. I now had one husband, two young sons who I was trying to keep as healthy as possible with lots of great home cooking, and my job as a medical director that I was very passionate about-I thought this was my life work. Oh, and have I mentioned yet that I was a consummate perfectionist? I pushed and pushed to get it all done and my own needs to nurture and care for myself usually came last.

The hospital laid me off due to budget cuts and I started a new consulting firm with a friend doing outcomes measurement for health and human service organisations. I was headed straight for a case of adrenal fatigue, which of course I didn't know existed because it isn't in the conventional medical paradigm I was trained in. I had low blood pressure, I couldn't stay warm, and I was fatigued. My answer was to start an intensive fitness program to get in better shape. I joined my boys at their dojo and trained to get my black belt in karate. I did accomplish this and soon after our whole family moved across town to live with my husband's sweet mother who was at this time confined to a wheelchair living with the end stages of Huntington's disease.

Needing to do frequent wheelchair transfers with my mother-in-law was the straw that tweaked this camel's back straight into chronic low back pain. After endless chiropractic adjustments, massages, and acupuncture, and searching for answers for why none of these provided permanent relief, I found Egoscue therapy and realized how out of alignment my whole body was. I thought I stood straight and tall but in fact my toes went out, my shoulders were slumped forward, my hip flexor muscles were tight and not engaging and my pelvis was rotated. Those wheelchair transfers weren't the cause of back having chronic pain, just the things that pushed it over the edge.

I became devoted to my daily postural exercises and my body slowly started to regain much better alignment. I was able to ditch the orthotics (in fact my body was quite adamant I not wear them) and the back pain subsided a lot as long as I did my daily exercises. My mother-in-law also was working with the same therapist and her body straightened out to a remarkable degree. I learned that bodies are designed to heal. If you give your body the correct movement and postural exercises, tremendous change and improvement in function is possible. Something else I hadn't learned in medical school.

At this point I had earned my black belt and traded training in the dojo, for training in how to care for someone with a degenerative illness confined to a wheelchair. Not to mention trying to find help in our quest to get her out of the wheelchair. The boys were now in high school and I wasn't playing chauffer, but the teenage years have their own set of stressors for kids and parents and we were not immune. Still pushing hard to do it all. Even though I had now figured out that a lot of my symptoms were due to adrenal fatigue, I still refused to let go of my constant push to do more.

My mother-in-law died peacefully one day. She had been able to take a few steps in the pool and I guess she figured at age 90 she had proved her point has taught me what I needed to know, so decided to go on to other adventures. Along the way I closed my consulting business and was now ramping up my healing practice and trying to learn how to do business online in the age of computers. Convinced I couldn't slow down, there was nothing on my plate I would let myself stop doing. Still pushing hard to do it all and do it all perfectly.

The Wheels Come of the Bus

Even though I tried to convince myself I was doing everything 'right', eating a healthy diet, doing my exercises, avoiding toxins as much as possible and doing my healing work, I still had not slowed down. Finally, my body started to have major tantrums to get my attention. First it was six months of severe chronic nerve pain in my right arm that left me unable to use the arm and having to learn to use my computer one handed. I had tried all my usual therapies to no avail but finally found a naturopath who did some visceral manipulation on my gall bladder and that did the trick. Once again, not something I learned in medical school.

Next up my low back and left sacroiliac joint went into revolt. Just seized up to the point I could not walk or stand without severe pain. For two months, I was able to do little else besides my Egoscue exercises, water therapy, healing work and rest. I learned a huge lesson in being grateful for the simple little everyday things. The first day I could stand at my sink and wash the dishes I was overcome with gratitude for that simple pleasure I usually grumbled over at worst and took for granted at best. On my healing journey, I was then led to a do an elimination diet that had me tossing all sugar-including fruit, grains and a bunch of other things my body didn't want when I bothered to ask it. This included all those healthy carrots I had been juicing - my body said no. All the remaining aches and pains in my back went away, whoa, I had no idea my diet was partly responsible for my SI joint pain - yep you guessed it, not something I learned in medical school.

With all these clues, it was harder and harder to ignore my need to slow down and I started to seriously try to prune back all this doing. Just in case, my body had one more major lesson for me. My gall bladder started to scream for attention—think incredibly painful gallbladder attacks. I do not take pain meds and I was not going to have my sweet little gall bladder removed, which is what I had learned was the answer to gall bladder attacks in medical school. Back to the drawing board. Fortunately, I found a chiropractor to help me fine-tune my diet, get on just the supplements my body needed and support the detoxing. Result? Gall bladder healing nicely, no more pain.

My Secret Weapon

Through all these twists and turns, I have learned to seriously listen to my body, to decrease the stress by doing what is important and letting the other stuff go and to stop striving to be perfect. I am getting better and better at loving myself for being just the way I am, which is NOT perfect. I continue to be okay with learning from the trouble spots in my life and continuing to heal my unconscious blocks—those traumas that are long buried in my past and keep me out of living in the flow.

During my explorations into alternative healing, I worked for some years with a group that researched consciousness. What I learned is that it is possible to heal anything, as long as you can leverage your consciousness and release the blocks your unconscious is putting in your way. This is incredibly powerful, to understand that you have all the power you need to accomplish whatever you want. No one 'out there' is holding you back, even though looking through the lens of your trauma might make it seem so. When I grasped this truth, I was hooked. No more feeling the powerless victim, healing was a matter of having the courage to look inside at the places of stored fear and other uncomfortable emotions and being committed to letting them go. That has been the biggest support and the most amazing tool, the healing work I have learned to do in my unconscious. I realize that I am the only one who holds myself back—not because I am incapable, but because parts of my unconscious are stuck in the past and are scared to move forward.

My Keys to a Life Full of Health and Vitality

Health is hugely important in all our lives. Anyone who has struggled with a chronic illness knows the immense impact on the ability to function in life. Health challenges affect our ability to be mothers, partners and to live our purpose in the world. In my journey as a healer to date I have come to believe that anyone can change their situation for the better—healing is always possible. You are either moving toward or away from wellness with the choices you make.

In looking for a framework for going on a healing journey, I have defined five pillars that support your ability to live a life of health and vitality.

First, is your commitment to health, without making this commitment to invest your time and resources nothing else will happen.

The second pillar is the need for a supportive diet. Notice I did not say a healthy diet. Every one of us has individual nutrient needs depending on our unique physiology and what is happening in our bodies from a health perspective. What is healthy food for one person may be very detrimental for someone else. Hence the need to eat food and take supplements that support your body to heal. This is definitely not one size fits all.

The third pillar is to adopt a healing lifestyle. The main components of this are getting ample sleep, decreasing exposure to toxins, increasing your body's detox capability and decreasing your stress load. This can seem daunting at first, but as these changes support an increase in vitality, they soon become no brainers.

The fourth pillar is working to improve your body alignment and engaging in supportive movement. Frequently, a sedentary lifestyle without enough supportive movement leads to postural misalignment, a body that can't function without pain and an increased risk of injury. Getting that healthy alignment back, and feeding your joints and muscles with supportive movement is helpful in so many ways.

The fifth pillar is leveraging consciousness. This pillar is the one that eases your way when inner resistance to making changes threatens to derail your progress. Learning and using a healing tool to release your inner unconscious blocks is the secret weapon that will support you when you struggle with the other pillars. I couldn't have made it to this point without it.

Heed the Advice of Your Flight Attendant

It took me quite a while to learn that I need to put my oxygen mask on first before helping someone near me who needs assistance. If I push too hard and take care of everyone else before myself, I don't have the energy to help others, be they family, friends or clients. The fastest way forward to successfully reaching your goals is to nurture and love yourself first. That way you have the energy, health and vitality to do whatever you want. When your body is functioning well, you are vastly more productive and effective.

If you are determined to step out and live your purpose big and bold in the world, take care of your most priceless asset, yourself. Commit to your health, support it with a healing lifestyle and get the assistance you need to leverage your consciousness and remove any unconscious internal blocks standing in your way.

From My Heart to Yours,

Dr. Mary

ABOUT THE AUTHOR

Dr. Mary Pellicer is an American physician, healer and teacher. Her lifelong commitment to healing work was inspired at age eight, when she witnessed the health ravages in Morocco while living there with her family.

Dr. Mary went to medical school and became a family physician. She started practice in a migrant health clinic but became frustrated with the conventional medical model and its limited ability to catalyze wellness.

Her journey of discovery from doctor to healer, had stopped as medical director of a healthy community program, as an outcomes measurement specialist and working with an international group researching consciousness. Dr. Mary is now in a practice with her sister, Cate, who is a holistic nutrition therapist. They use their combined expertise to assist people struggling with autoimmune conditions. Dr. Mary is passionately committed to the art of healing and believes in the possibility of healing--healing no matter what.

Agnese Osemwegie- This is My Story

"To me, leadership is about encouraging people. It's about stimulating them. It's about enabling them to achieve what they can achieve - and to do that with a purpose" - Christine Lagarde

I will share my life experiences here as I believe that this will help and change someone's life. The reason why I am openly sharing is that I believe my life is the only currency I have, to help to other working mothers and wives.

Whatever I do or prepare to do, I will always dig deep and question until the roots, much deeper than people normally do, as I know that key for everything in life is hidden in original root, foundation and purpose, whether it is relationships, work, kids, political issues, business, family or health.

I grew up in Latvia which is in Eastern Europe; I lived in a home where domestic violence by my stepdad to my mother was almost an everyday occurrence. Up to today, my mother still inspires me when I think about how she overcame those difficulties and remains such a sweet, kind, responsible and gentle person. Her example shaped me as a person and taught me that I do not have to allow circumstances to dictate who I am, but I dictate who I am through the wise choices I make every day in what I think, say and do.

However, as a result of the challenges I had growing up, it made it hard for me to understand what it means to have a strong and healthy family with a wise and responsible man as the head of the home and also how I could retain my identity as a woman. This internal conflict was bothering me for years, especially when I came to the age when I was ready to get married.

During these difficult times, I was looking for my purpose and in 2003, I accepted Jesus as my Lord and Saviour and surrendered my life to Him. My life changed supernaturally, my perspective became transformed. Those who saw my life before and after this event, many of them also gave their lives to Jesus.

Around this time, I started my own little business, everything I prayed for was answered, but then I felt the urge to travel to England and no one that knew me could not understand my decision, as usually people from Latvia travelled to earn money by doing menial jobs, which was not the case for me as my business was growing.

Despite many pleas to reconsider, I travelled to the UK for the summer. When the summer finished I had a ticket back, but for some reason I wanted to stay. All of the time, I had questions in my heart such as 'what is the purpose for my life'?

I liked England a lot and wanted to stay there and start the same business what I was doing back home, but I could not, as my knowledge of the system of the country, language skills, and the fact that, if it fails, I had nowhere to fall back upon. So at that time I asked God to answer three prayers for me. These prayers were to help me determine if it was His will for me to be in the UK, then if so, I needed to see His support.

Firstly, I asked God for a husband in whose life, God is the priority, as I knew that according to the original foundations, the husband usually carries direction. The second that God increases my wages to double what I was earning at the time. Thirdly, God had to make a way so I can get into university, which was outrageous as my

English language skills were not good at all.

During this period, I met my husband. It was my second most important appointment in my life. He became my teacher, encourager, protector, guide and leader! Finally, I understood why God said, 'is not a good person to be alone'. Whatever I mentioned I wanted to do, he was always pushing me for it and made me believe that I can do whatever I put my mind to do. He revealed for me Gods depths and lengths. He saw me as a rough diamond, which needs to be polished to shine! Within the year after that prayer all three my prayers were answered. Additionally, I passed successfully also all my official exams in University, (listed in top 20 university list in England), so I studied part time and also got a job in the Civil Service in London where my salary not only was doubled, but nearly tripled. Despite my language skills, I passed my driving test, and, yes, that all happened within one year after my prayer.

When I met my husband, he said something in one of our first dates that confirmed to me that this is my husband indeed and that I can finally be who God made me be in totality. He said to me, that 'I want a wife that is a partner to me in everything that I do and I do not want a wife that is simply a cook and a cleaner'. This became a conviction in our hearts about how we desired to live our lives. Our minds expanded through finding out the truth about God's original intention of creating a man and woman.

Discovering the original foundations how things were created in a beginning is the key to success for our family, business, relationships, for me personally as a wife, mother and also daughter. We discovered that there are no limits of how far humans can go and achieve. That there is a purpose for every individual on this planet and you can go as far as your mind can stretch.

Nevertheless, our desire was not easily achievable, because when we got married and started living under the same roof, we started fighting and discovered many imperfections about each other. I became pregnant with our first child while working on our vision and our company's development. Then I got pregnant with the second child, but our character problems brought a lot of distractions, stress and mess in our marriage, work and our home. Our work was disturbed every day and because the children were small, I could not figure out a strategy to manage work, home, children and my relationship with my husband.

We could not understand how two people who loved God and loved each other so much can fight and be so disorganised. All we knew was what we wanted but we did not know how, as our reality was opposite from what was the will of God for us.

What we did not know then, but know now, is that success in anything is as a result of following the correct laws and principles. There are laws and principles about money, marriage, children, healthy spiritual life, and health, so on, while failure is simply the inability or unwillingness to apply the correct principles and laws. As laws will work against the person, or they will help them, the same as the law of gravity, no matter how good or bad a person may be.

Even if we were thinking that we own the world and that we will transform the world, but we discovered, that no matter how stretched our minds was and no matter how motivated we were, we understood that we were actually not going anywhere without first fixing ourselves from inside as we were violating every law for successful living. We understood, that if we cannot be faithful over the little given to us, how can we get something more.

Around this time, God spoke to my husband that we need to move to Latvia. He knew my Pastor from the church where I got saved and when we moved, it was just exactly we were praying for, we discovered that our purpose without characters could not be reached. That was something very amazing for me to see how my husband was led by God and I was glad that I obeyed my husband's voice.

Our Pastor laid the foundations that were missing, especially through an incredible leadership course, which changed our entire lives. He focused on the character, purpose of man and showed and thought us HOW it works in practice. We learnt how to achieve the specific goals, how to identify the direction in life and business, how to strategize and plan life a-z, how to structure every minute in the day. He transferred various ingenious ways how we can make our unlimited dreams real and practically achievable not just in theory. Even my husband, with his impressive biography of many degrees, courses, his background as a university lecturer and even advisory background, were surprised about this course, how life transforming it was.

After this, we knew exactly what we needed to do and how. Our marriage gradually improved and our lives began to come together just like the pieces of a puzzle. As a result of God's incredible guidance, today we own some companies including a further education college. We help people around the world to build businesses, we are home-schooling our children, we also teach people how to achieve their goals, set up direction, and through our work we are passing to others everything we have learned over the years.

Every woman is uniquely gifted by the providence of God to be her husband's helper in all that he does, because men in general think of straight lines and this are good for building structures whether it is family structure, organisational structures and so on. A woman on the other hand is more intuitive, relationship focused, natural planner and can fill the gaps to make every endeavor successfully to happen.

Example years ago, when we first began working in the business together, my husband pitched a business concept to a company and they said: 'send us your offer in writing'. So, my husband will write out the concept, we both agree the pricing and strategy how it will work and then I will create a very professional presentation and send it off. In subsequent meetings, people always commented on how impressive our materials looked and it was always interesting for me, as I never studied graphic design and sales skills in school, but because this was something that me and my husband were working on, these dynamic pulled things out of me that I did not know within me.

Another example. Years ago, I never could have imagined, that we will own a further education college. During my years of home-schooling my children, and helping my husband by directing and managing the courses in which he was teaching investors and business professionals in, I learned a lot. Especially as we were building our first company together from scratch. Today, when I manage the school, all of my previous experiences, learned strategies from my incredible husband and from my Pastor Rufus Ajiboye (who have become as my father), not only have given me the confidence to make things happen and to manage our businesses, but also have given me ability to teach and to pass to others all I have learned myself during the years.

This scenario plays out in every area of our lives whereby we always try to work as true partners; this works well not only in the business, but also in the kitchen, children education, ministry and so on. There are a set direction and a plan that we both participate in doing together.

We also delegate people, we split the tasks. Nothing is impossible for our team, as we have an understanding of the original foundations and our direction and purpose for our family.

We always comment on how much talents and gifts lie within women who feel that the fact that they are wives and mums, excludes them from contributing to society in a meaningful manner. We believe that, it is such a colossal waste for us to educate girls, train them only for them to be left at home later for the best years of their lives. Mums in business, does not mean that the children are neglected, but it means that the family has found their purpose and that a woman has a fundamental shift in thinking and determination to make it happen. To integrate the kids within this structure and vision as they grow up, will fill their lives with dynamism and will set an example for them for life, especially my two daughters, my example is teaching them how to be practically a woman of purpose and vision.

Therefore, my advice to women will always be to do business and to structure it around their lives. Achieving the right balance is not very easy, but remember, where is a will, there is a way!

I want to share with you core inspiration that transformed my life. What I will share with you, gave me a powerful ''kick' in the back to step up to take a role of a wife, a mother and a leader that I originally was created to be. So back to foundations!

Proverbs 31 woman from the bible is more than the ideal wife and mother. She is my inspiration and a role model for modern day mom entrepreneurs – sharing her gifts and talents, working long hours and sharing the wisdom and compassion at home, in her business and her community, setting a practical example for her children and workers.

- She supports her husband: Prov 31:11 "The heart of her husband trusts in her, and he will have no lack of gain."

- With her entrepreneurial nature, she is putting her talents and skills at work, her business successfully bears fruits: Prov 31:13-14 ''She seeks wool and flax, and works with willing hands. She is like the ships of the merchant; she brings her food from afar."

- She contributes not only to the welfare of her children but also to her workers and to her entire household: Prov 31:15 "She gets up while it is still dark; she provides food for her family and portions for her servant girls."

- She makes wise business decisions and invests her profits in the future: Prov 31:16 "She inspects a field and buys it. With her earnings, she plants a vineyard."

- She provides for her family with an entrepreneurial spirit and a dedication to her work. Prov 31:18

"She sees her trading is profitable, and her lamp does not go out at night."

- From all that is given to her, she changes lives for others: Prov 31:20 ''She opens her hand to the poor and reaches out her hands to the needy.''

- She lives with purpose and is prepared for the future: Prov 31:21 "When it snows, she has no fear for her household; for all of them are clothed in scarlet."

- She is a wise teacher and mentor: Prov 31:26 "She speaks with wisdom and faithful instruction is on her tongue."

- All of her hard work not only sets an example, but also earns her praise and respect: Prov 31:28 "Her children arise to call her blessed: her husband also, and he praises her."

- She is the supermum and superwife: Prov 31:29 "Many women do noble things, but you surpass them all."

- She is rewarded because of her faith – because she honors, loves and respects the Lord: Prov 31:30"Charm is deceptive, and beauty is fleeting; but a woman who fears the Lord is to be praised."

So, when Creator released a manual of what should come out of His created beauty, then I am and you should be confident to trust your Creator, who knows best.

Pursuing the ultimate purpose in your life will make you also very satisfied. When I was unclear about my purpose, my Pastor asked me: 'Agnese, what are your satisfactions in life, assess yourself'' and my answer was "to break lies and to establish the truth and then to see people live to change!"

This is the reason I have agreed to share my story. I am not going to just drop the story and leave, but I will give you an opportunity to contact me so that I can use what is given to me to help you structure your life, as I know that to change an established reality is not easy by yourself and always you will need someone, the same way that I had someone who helped me to change my life, and whatever has been given to me, I will give it to you and your life will never stay the same I can guarantee you that. My highest satisfaction is to see women and families transformed around the world. Just write me a letter: www.evagoglobal.com/contact-us

ABOUT THE AUTHOR

Agnese is the dynamic Co-Founder and Chief Operating Officer of an investment banking company Evago Global Capital, co-owner of a Further Education College, both located in Riga Latvia, founded by her and her husband Evans Osemwegie. Coming from a background in the Civil Service in London, she left it to pursue her and her husband's vision of launching EGC. Over the years, she has played a key role in the growth of the company. Additionally, Agnese is passionate about changing people lives, by helping individuals to find their purpose in life. She is a natural motivator and extremely passionate about entrepreneurship, because she believes that this is the way that people can maximize God given talents and gifts to transform the world. She is naturally gifted in sales and marketing, highly creative and able to find new solutions to complex problems. Agnese is also a passionate Christian and credits God as the source of everything she is, has achieved and will achieve in life. Everything that she does is based on God's values. She has devoted wife and treasures her relationships with her husband, children and parents who all are her team members. Additionally, she is a devoted mum to three amazing children, her son and two daughters.

Franscica Okin - My Journey So Far

"Success is... knowing your purpose in life, growing to reach your maximum potential, and sowing seeds that benefit others"
-John C. Maxwell

I met my husband on one of our group outings in my nurse's hostel in 1975. He was also a student studying at Bolton College of Technology, we started dating and I noticed we had a few things in common, like going to the cinema and music. After dating for while I introduced him to my brother who was also studying at that time, all went well and I knew it would lead to marriage. Our relationship progressed as I wanted it to be and we eventually got married in 1978. Oh, happy day.

After a year, my husband went back to Nigeria to serve the country in a scheme called National Youth Service Corps, before he left he made it clear he was not a fan of the cold weather and will not be coming back, at that point I knew I would eventually have to go back home so we could live and enjoy our marriage as husband and wife. With everything going on around me, I had our first daughter, another happy day.

After completion of my nursing program I prepared to travel back to Nigeria with my daughter, my husband had not met her and he was so excited and looking forward to seeing her. I arrived in Nigeria with joy and hope to be reunited my husband, it was a great feeling to be reunited again.

After the settling period was over, I applied for a job and started my career as a staff nurse with various private hospitals and I rose to the position of a matron after several years of work experience. I had the privilege to meet many big personalities and state governors in Nigeria as they patronized the hospital I was working in.

As a registered nurse and midwife with many years of working experience, I look at my life and I am filled with gratitude, I have had the opportunity work across various options in my nursing career like medical, surgical and maternity. My most recent experience is working in the renounced National Hospital for Neurology and Neurosurgery which specializes in all aspects of neurological conditions including stroke and traumatic brain injury.

Nursing as a career has been my choice since I was a child, after helping to look after my grandma who was bedridden with stroke and was nursed at home until her demise. My parents wanted me to study to become a doctor because I was very good at sciences and obtained Grade 1 in my final exams at a school in 1969; but I choose to nurse. My passion for nursing made my parents send me to the UK in 1973 to pursue my passion. When I look at some of my certificates like Registered Manager Award, Family Planning Practitioner and Specialist Neurological Nursing just to mention a few, I am glad and pleased my achievements. I am a devout Christian with three beautiful daughters and eight grandchildren, at this point I will like to mention that my first daughter is the complier of this amazing anthology and I am so proud of her and her works.

Life as a working mom

It was quite a busy and demanding time for me, taking the children to the daycare centre and going to work as my husband leaves home very early in the morning for work. When my second daughter arrived, I took time off work to look after my children; my mother was very helpful and supportive with childcare and house chores.

Life as a mother

My profession demands me to be on my feet most of the day, and by the time I get home I am tired and exhausted. That never stops me from catching up with my children, it is always a pleasure looking after them and watching them grow, monitoring their educational and spiritual growth. A very demanding task for me, I recall caring for my children, cooking, laundry, shopping, sleepless nights to care for them when sick which reminds me of this song "My Mother who sat and watched my infant head, when sleeping on my cradle bed".

Motherhood is an experience that no one can explain to you except you pass through the phase of pregnancy, birth, childhood, adolescence to adulthood. One of my keys to success is knowing that I am only a custodian of my children. So, I have a responsibility to train them in the fear of the Lord, to mold them early to what I want them to be so that I can enjoy the later part of my life in peace, joy and love.

How things changed and how I made it work

I fell into a vicious circle of going to work, caring for my children and did not even have time to look after myself and was always burnt out at the end of the day. I had to do something different so I could get better results. I sat down and drew an up timetable for myself on my daily activities and rescheduled most of my daily house chores like laundry, got myself live-in house help and arranged with the nursery to bring my children home after school with the school bus. I had a day off to go out to visit friends and family or watch a movie with my husband. I arranged with my hairdresser to come weekly to dress my hair at home. This new schedule freed me up and gave me time back. I realised there is a need to prioritise work, manage children and to remain happy. As my children grew up, the process became easier and had more freedom to do more of what I wanted to do.

Right Now

I wanted to come back to the UK but delayed it for my children's sake, when my youngest daughter gained admission to the university; I summoned up courage and went after my goal. I applied for a job from Nigeria to the UK and the whole process went smoothly. I arrived back to the UK and continued with my passion for working with people. My first daughter eventually came to join me in the UK in 2004 and I had good company till she got her first job and relocated to another town. We kept in touch throughout this period; she continued to progress with her life and got married. She is settled with her husband and two children in the M4 Corridor area. My other daughters are also doing well as well, happily married with children in Nigeria.

I am enjoying my life right now, enjoying each day as it comes. Doing things, I love and enjoy from watching movies to spending quality time with my grandchildren, here in the UK and Nigeria. I am focusing my energy on things that matter and leaving minor things alone; for example, if I can't cook because my body is tired, I order in a take away. My life is simpler and richer the moment I finally permitted myself to be. In closing to all busy working mothers reading this, know that you are valuable, know that you matter. Take care of yourself because you are worth it. Spend quality time to relax and rejuvenate, be kind to yourself, treat yourself and enjoy your life.

ABOUT THE AUTHOR

Franscica Okin is a Registered Nurse in the UK, enjoying spending time with her children and grandchildren in the UK and Nigeria.

Part Four:
Making My Mark

THE PURPOSE DRIVEN LADY- OLAJUMOKE POKU

From the online magazine, The Purpose Driven Lady Issue 5

Please tell us a bit about yourself? Who are you? What do you do?

My name is Olajumoke Poku preferably called Jummy by families and friend. I am married with two beautiful children. I am a social worker in the adult services.

What is one thing people would be surprised to know about you?

Oh, how I love to dance to contemporary music in traditional African dance style… oops!

What is a typical day like for you?

I'm an early riser, I am usually out of bed about 5 am to spend quality time with God. I am a mother of two school age children, so I get them ready and drop off to school. As a full time working professional, I'm at work for the whole working day, and back home in the evening for family time.

What does purpose mean to you? Do you know your purpose? What is your purpose?

The purpose for me is what I'm on earth for. Primarily, I am here as God's creation to enjoy his creation. I know who I am in Christ and I know I'm set within his will. My purpose is multi-faceted. However, one thing is clear; I am here as an ambassador of Christ to be who and what HE would have me be, and do what HE would have me do. For instance, I am a child of God, daughter to my parents, sisters to my siblings, a friend that sticks closer to my friends, wife to my husband, mother to my children, minister in the body of Christ as a whole and so much more. In each role and with each responsibility I fulfil the purpose for which I will give an account for in the end.

Could you please share how you are using your purpose? Do you have any regrets?

Oh no! I don't do regrets; even when I fail, I learn from it and pick myself back up. I fulfil God's purpose daily for everyone I come in contact with. I ensure I make a positive impression on them. In the "church sense" of using purpose I am a teacher of God's word, I am passionate about God's word, inspiring women to stand strong as pillars in their home and hold on to God's word for all things.

At present, God gave me a burden and mission to intercede for the body of Christ and proclaim the return of the Lord Jesus Christ our King. My prayer is that there will be an awakening in the body of Christ and the church of God will become eternally focused.

How has your relationship with God played a role in your success so far?

I am nothing without God and He alone has kept me this far. My success is Christ Himself and He alone owns the credit to how far I have come in life.

What quote do you live by? Who are your heroes?

Unfortunately, I don't live by quotes... LOL; I live by God's word alone. I have been inspired by so many ministers over the years, starting with Kenneth E Hagin, Myles Munroe, Joyce Meyer, John MacArthur, Max Lucado and lots more.

What is the ultimate dream/goal for you?

To be ready and make it back home to Jesus empty! Having fulfilled all He has called me to do.

In closing, what three things would you encourage women to do more than of?

You can't love enough, love God with all your heart, soul and spirit. And love anyone God brings across your way; only through love can the gospel and truth of Christ be revealed.

Pray like nothing else matters and depend on God's word more than anything else; know God all by yourself.

ABOUT THE AUTHOR

I am a mum wife, Christian woman with a passion for God's word and excellence in our ways to honour God. I strive to reach out to others and I encourage positive thinking. Friends say she is a woman after God's own heart, a good listener, always having words of encouragement when you need one. Most of all she loves God and it shows in everything she does.

DIARY OF A PURPOSE DRIVEN LADY WITH BUKOLA ORAGBADE

It's 11:40pm. My head finally gets to hit the pillow and as I said, "Thank you Holy Spirit for today", a question came to mind, was today a Mary or Martha day?

Luke 10:41-42(NLT) But the Lord said to her, "My dear Martha, you are worried and upset over all these details! 42: There is only one thing worth being concern about. Mary has discovered it, and it will not be taken away from her."

Well, we woke up late earlier that day and had to rush through getting the children ready for school. I put my six-year-old daughter's hair in a bun, while she was eating breakfast and hubby were wearing her shoes for her at the same time. My nine-year-old asked the same question at the door that he asks every day, 'Mummy, can I walk to school by myself?' And he got the same answer he gets every day. NO! (The school is a three-minute walk from the house)

This would all have been easier if my eighteen-month-old had still been in bed, but there she was, clinging to my side and calling me Daddy. I have been trying to get her to say mummy since she started talking! Sigh.

Finally, they were gone. Breakfast. What will I have for breakfast? I have been trying to go on a "low carb" diet. How hard can that be? The little bulge after my third baby is taking its time to budge! No bread, no rice, no fried plantain (seriously, my favourite carb too?) Today was just not the day! I had my bread and egg without blinking...lol

I had a prayer time for thirty minutes with hubby, then off to the library to prepare for an exam, gym then home. We all know what happens when Momma gets home? Everyone wants a piece of her! Finally, they are in bed and I'm picking up this and that, sweeping here and there, wondering why hubby is fixated on the Presidential debate and not noticing the hard work I'm putting in

STEP OUT

(who sent me right?)

Finally, in bed and I jumped up remembering the clothes I wanted to put in the washing machine...ugh!! Rush down and back to bed...that was when the thought began, a Mary or Martha day?

We all remember the story of how Mary sat learning at the feet of Jesus or in the time and age, I could call it doing "Spiritual stuff" i.e. Reading or studying the word, meditating, praying etc.

Well that's the summary of MY day, yours might be similar, simpler, or more complicated but two important things to note is that whatever season of life you are in is never void of the 'busyness' that comes with that season and there is wisdom available for every season of life.

Don't feel bad about the season you're in. Guilt will not take you anywhere; find a way to incorporate prayer time, study time & meditation in the season you are in.

Today I spent some time while in the library walking around and speaking the word of God under my breath, over some areas of my life.

I'll like to share some wisdom I've used over the years. I believe as you yield to the Holy Spirit, He'll give you the specific understanding for your season in life.

I used to spend my break time at work taking a walk and praying in the spirit (looking back now, I'm sure many people tagged me weird!) Well, I'll rather be Weird Mary sitting at His feet than Confused Martha wasting time away with my colleagues!

One of my greatest assets is my iPhone and earpiece, not because it hooks me up to Facebook, Instagram, Twitter and Google but because it unhooks me from my surroundings when needed! Did you know that the bible app could read the bible to you? You can listen to the bible on the train to work, while cooking, cleaning and at the hairdressers, oh yes you can!

1.Find people in the same season as you are, two is better than one the bible says, (Ecclesiastes 4:9) When I was looking for a job, I spoke to someone in that same season of life. We made plans and started meeting on Face Time, Monday to Friday for an hour praying, casting our cares & worries on God.

Ask questions, seek knowledge. I read this quote somewhere, 'It's best if you don't have all the answers' Where you are now, many have been and passed through! There is no need to re-invent the wheel, learn from the experience of others.

2. Ask the Holy Spirit for Wisdom: What works for me will certainly not work for you, but the Holy Spirit will give you insight into ways you can reduce the busyness and incorporate study, prayer and meditation into your life. There are days I have had to order food from a caterer, hire someone to clean the house and the one I love most is disposables, plates, spoons etc Just eat and bin! Praise the Lord for that…lol

STEP OUT

My kids have a fair share of their chores; we tend to forget how old we were when we started chores. My nine-year-old takes the bin out, hoovers and supervises his little sister (He loves the supervisory role best...lol)

Someone once said that if you chase perfection, you set yourself up for disappointment! Some days, the wisdom might be, leave it all alone and go to bed! Give yourself a break; focus on the main thing, be a Mary in Martha's world.

3. Don't give up: Some days you get it right, and someday you don't! Some days you planned to pray for an hour and the best you did was muttered, thank you Jesus, as you dragged your body to bed! God is not a Chief Whip, waiting for you to fail. He yearns to fellowship with you more than you know. The days you read a verse and the days you read five chapters; He is still crazy about you.

God's love for you, is not based on what you do but on what He has done, don't take the pressure that comes with living in Martha's world, His grace is available for you today Embrace it!

ABOUT THE AUTHOR

Buki Oragbade is a Pastor at Kingsword International Church Chicago. She loves writing in her spare time. She is married to Pastor Dotun Oragbade and they have three beautiful kids. They reside in Wilmette, Illinois.

Aminat Alli - My Beautiful Scar

"Everything in this life has a purpose, there are no mistakes, no coincidences" - *Elisabeth Kubler-Ross*

Most often in life, you allow circumstances beyond your scope to define you which is not the best considering the negativity that results from it especially when a scar is involved. Depending on the book or website you check, the definition of a scar varies but points to the same meaning. According to dictionary.com, a scar is a mark left by a healed wound, sore or burn (I refer to this as a physical scar) or a lasting effect of trouble or psychological injury as a result of suffering (I refer to this as an emotional scar). So that means a scar can be physical or emotional.

Emotional scars tend to control us the most, because only the individual knows it's there. It's like a bomb on a timer, it ticks and tocks every second and could lead to an explosion. It's only a matter of time, especially if not handled properly. It is like a curtain hiding a whole lot of insecurity, behind it a whole lot of untold stories, layers of bottled up feelings and an injury to the soul. Some deep, others shallow. Some heal over time and could be filed under bittersweet memories, while others become the baggage that wrecks future joy. Today I want to talk about the physical scar, the one seen and talked about by others.

I remember having an appendectomy when I was in my teen, some complications resulted in me staying at the hospital over a month and when I was discharged, it was with a very funny scar on my stomach. I call it funny because of the comments I get when people see it. The kindest comment I got was that the doctor must have been annoyed with me. I became very self-conscious for a long time I hated exposing the scar; it was an additional flaw to a long list of flaws I had mentally put together as a teenager. Over a time, as I was growing up, maturity sets in I finally realised the symbolism of the scar. My matured self-realised that the scar was preparing me for the future.

STEP OUT

Let me explain…

I am married to the sweetest man ever and was blessed with the fruit of the womb within the first year of our marriage and it was a beautiful experience. My pregnancy was crisis free thank God. My husband was an angel. My family (immediate, in-laws and friends) were my rock. I had all the support a first-time mom could ask for.

On the D-Day, my water broke very early in the morning, I was happy at first because I was looking forward to being a mom, then reality set in, to be a biological mom means a visit to the delivery room. Being a first-time mom, I have listened, googled, watched, read and almost overdosed on any information about delivery and newborns and to be honest, I was scared of what goes on in the delivery room, especially all that could go wrong. I was filled with fear that grew as I approached the hospital. My mind became a movie set with a background running commentary about all that could go wrong (not a good thing at all). Fear was taking over; I had to put a stop to it quickly by reminding myself of God's favour during the pregnancy. With that thought I entered the delivery room.

After about thirty-six hours I was taken to the theater for a caesarian section. I had a great team that attended to me; they were doing their job very well. For me it was an honor to be taken care of by them especially professionally and efficiently. After delivery, lo and behold another scar to contend with but this time

I embraced it wholeheartedly.

I called it "My Beautiful Scar", a badge of honor, whenever I feel it; I am overwhelmed with emotions. I feel this sense of pride rise up within me. I came. I saw. I conquered. My beautiful scar became a daily reminder of God's favor upon me. When I look at the gift bestowed on me through this process, my daughter (a diamond that will sparkle forever by God's Grace) my conviction is definite. I will gladly do this all over again. Scars come in different ways and circumstances, how you handle it is what makes the difference.

The first scar I had prepared me for the second scar. It made me realise whatever happens in life, a purpose is attached even if I don't know it yet. Now there is always this deep and complete gratitude to God on a daily basis for my beautiful scar. It is a symbol of strength, of motherhood, of a battle won on my behalf by the Almighty, of prayers answered.

My approach to my second scar "My Beautiful Scar" as I call it now has made me acknowledge God's Grace in my life. I want to encourage you to approach your scar from a positive angle; different from the way you have been doing and watch your transformation as God's love supersedes all principalities. Thank you

ABOUT THE AUTHOR

Aminat Alli is a wife and mom who loves seeing the funny side of life and is allergic to pretense and hypocrisy. Professionally a pharmacist, believes in God first and every other thing falls in place.

Conclusion

I hope you have enjoyed reading this book as much as the busy working mothers who have taken time to share their stories with you. Through the pages I hope you have come to see that you too can leave your best live, that you can achieve that goal and live your dream.

Not many busy working mothers were bold enough to share their experiences and bare as much as for the great of good, so that another mother can find the answers she is seeking.

I hope that you have come to realise that you too can step out and release your inner greatness.

I hope you will pursue your passion so that you can ultimately experience fulfilment and live the life that you love.

Thank you for reading Step Out Book I would love to hear from you, please post a comment on Amazon or my facebook Omowunmi Olunloyo immediately to let me know how this book has helped you.

STEP OUT

Find me here

@OmowunmiOlunloyo
www.stepout.strikingly.com
www.omowunmiolunloyo.com
www.facebook.com/omowunmi.olunloyo
www.facebook.com/groups/BusyWorkingMom
https://www.facebook.com/OmowunmiToksOlunloyo

About the Compiler

Omowunmi Olunloyo, the founder of Create Your Reality and Find Your Place, Position & Purpose, is a top UK Women Empowerment Coach, International bestselling Author, Speaker and Mentor. She is committed to showing women especially busy working moms who feel stressed, overwhelmed and out of control in their life how to develop a road-map that supports them so that they can regain control of all aspects of their life and are fulfilled, happy and get better results in their life.

A plain spoken ever-bubbly coach, she supports clients to find clarity and direction in their lives. She empowers busy working mums who feel like their search for fulfillment is heading nowhere or no matter what they are doing their seed is not bearing fruit to become focused and start experiencing a lifestyle of ease, fulfillment and productivity.

Omowunmi Olunloyo or Toks as she is known as, is a dynamic speaker who has built her platform of purpose, possibility and power of the years of struggle with low self-esteem, not good enough and trying to fit in. Now a reformed intentional woman on purpose, free from condemnation, lack and self-worth, Toks uses her own story to motivate, encourage and empower other women. No more procrastination, No more excuses, No more delays, No MORE!

The recent launch of her online magazine – The Purpose Driven Lady is gaining grounds and becoming more popular. Like she always says" You are here once; you might as well live your best life ever". She lives in Burnham with her husband and their two children.

OTHER RESOURCES

Are you an overwhelmed, starting to worry busy working mom?

You might relate to some of these questions:

- Do you feel you have lost yourself?

- Do you have a big goal you want to achieve?

- Do you wake up every morning to go to a job that does nothing to fire you up?

- Do you ask yourself why some can live the life of their dreams and you can't?

- Do you want more for yourself? I can help you take the next step.

Introducing my transformational program called Personal Success Launchpad this is my proven 5 Steps to C.Y.O.R System to help busy working mothers just like you who are struggling with the overwhelm of managing family, job and other commitments and who feel unfulfilled with every day that passes like they're missing out on something valuable to discover and release their true inner greatness and regain total control of all aspects of their lives.

So, if you are ready to say goodbye to the Old You and embrace the New You that is living the kind of life that is intentionally on purpose with ease, go to www.omowunmiolunloyo.com to access my free checklist on How to Eliminate Frustration and Overwhelm & Start Experiencing a Lifestyle of Ease, Fulfillment & Productivity

More Books by Omowunmi Olunloyo

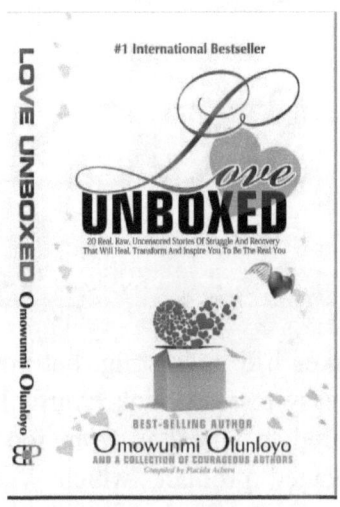

Open your heart to new possibilities and explore the stories in this book. You will find a treasure trove of real journeys, where you will discover answers to your questions about life and true happiness.

STEP OUT

Innovation makes life interesting, but not easy. In this powerful and easy-to-read book, you will find the key elements required to take you from food ideas, to an attractive packaged product, which will give you a competitive edge in the food manufacturing world.

STEP OUT

Have you ever wondered how to pray for your career, finances, family or life in general? Do you get stuck on what to say to God when you pray? Would you like to learn a simple formula that will allow you to see more answers to your prayers?

STEP OUT

The <u>Purpose Driven Lady Magazine</u> is for the lady who wants to be all that she has been created to be!

About the Publisher

Book Projects thanks you for reading Step Out: Release your inner greatness. Our mission is to support women to discover their innate potential through writing. We provide affordable book publishing and marketing. Our programs are designed to help women find courage, inspiration and encouragement to set themselves apart as they reach new heights.

We offer to coach, mentoring, and encourage building a supportive network, sharing stories and offering resources for lifestyle and business growth.

Working with us in a collaborative book is more than just writing a book. You come to write a book, you leave ready to soar. Your mind's eyes are opened to new possibilities. You are taken on a journey that expands not just your business but your future, creating a legacy for generations to come.

About our Books:

They are a collection of Life Journeys and Lessons learned. Life lessons are never learned in isolation. The contributors may be from different cultures, race and ethnicity, but they share in each other's joys and sorrows

Placid Acheru, the founder of Book Projects has helped 1000's of women providing a decade of coaching and mentoring experience. She is passionate about supporting women to become bestselling authors - the reason she created the #200womenauthors campaign. Placida is a Multi-award-winning business coach and Multi-time international bestselling author.

More about our publishing and marketing service can be found at:

Website: http://bookprojects.uk/
Twitter: https://twitter.com/Book_Projects

www.ingramcontent.com/pod-product-compliance
Lightning Source LLC
Chambersburg PA
CBHW030234170426
43201CB00006B/218